LIABLE PROMISES:

The Enabler of Conducts Universal and Evangelic

OLUSANYA KOLEOSHO

Cover designed by Cover Designer

This book draws from the author's Academic Investigation regarding some Ancient and Modern Exemplars of the Evangelical faith. Research subjects, characters, places, and incidents are products of the author's structured samplings from the Bible and the Biographical Christian Literatures. The Modern Exemplars as research subjects are excluded in the writing of this book.

Author: Olusanya Koleosho, MBA, PhD, CTFL, HCISPP

Printed in the United States of America

Third Printing: November 2020

Visit the *Liable Promises* book website –
https://hosanna-web-app.azurewebsites.net

ISBN- 978-1-7344711-1-3

CONTENTS

INTRODUCTION

A promise carries some credibility or misgivings to its audience. Reflecting on your present situation, you may be pursuing after a promise. Or, perhaps, you are pursuing nothing or having no idea of any influence. You may take a moment to do a review on yourself, as a giver or receiver of a promise. Upon becoming disinterested or skeptical, you may discover some subtle trade-off with another promise, parallel or opposing to your current position.

Consider or imagine the following frames of reference that can trigger some promise with orientations in opposing directions. The Dollar currency presents a note of promise on demand with a low or high interest rate with different effects on the creditors or the debtors, who mostly are in oblivion to the ascribed motto on it, "In God, We Trust." The Stock market trading, that goes up and down, presents a promise for the bear and another for the bull. Various Political persuasions have implied the same constitutional promise of a viable nation for votes and various movements. Social Media and Technology have promised the privacy status readily susceptible to some marketing exploits. Some Health Care interventions that promise the preventives or curatives apparently further hide some inherent adverse side effects. The thrill of the addicts has been drugs seductive to euphoria and suicide. The mitigation of business residual risks promised through the insurance coverage obscures the remote "acts of God." The polluting "acts of man" have been placed into a figurative 'world laboratory' which has promised the preservation of the world with human restraints, however, threatening the immediate human survival of some. The promise to control birth rate has been supplanted by generational atrophy in some nations requiring migrant populations as supplement. Some people groups with the promise of male preferred birth-controlled population, short of unmarried women, soon produce the longings for foreign women. Single, married or a divorcee respective beneficial advantages have their distinctive approvals or disapprovals in the same open culture. For many, adopting the promises of either the religious or the secular lifestyle still holds out for them life that is very uncertain until death. It is a valid assumption that parallel or opposing outlooks in life prevail from many liable promises.

The Biblical worldview reveals that the empirical world begins in the confines of the Edenic garden with a promise. Adam is promised life by not ingesting, or death by ingesting the biform fruit of the 'tree of knowledge of good and evil.' Then, the Devil contra-promises the couple by discounting the original promise, with the lofty promise, 'to be as gods,' to Adam and Eve who then distrust God by eating of the biform fruit resulting in the original spiritual death.

Considering the temptation narratives in the garden, you may want to take note of the startup of the cognitive rendezvous with humanity. The Devil questions Eve's cognition about God's promise regarding the tree of knowledge by asking "Has God indeed said, 'You shall not eat of every tree in the Garden?'" (Genesis 3:1 NKJV). In the same chapter 3 verse 9, after the fall of Adam and Eve, God questions the un-misled Adam by asking him to self-account *"Where* are you?" but in verse 13, God asks the misled Eve to define the naked outcome, *"What* is this you have done?" As in Blooms taxonomy, a cognitive entry level is indicated by the foremost question a learner asks regarding a given concept. Further questions asked in a stepwise order will advance the learner's knowledge on the concept. Literate or illiterate, the rational mind concept-queries self or others upward and stepwise with terms ranging from *What* (to define), *Which* (to comprehend), *When* (to apply), *Why* (to differentiate), *Where* (to synthesize), to *Whose* (to evaluate). Accordingly, the querying terms have been applied to instruct on the lifestyle effect of Liable Promises upon conviction. In going through each chapter and each section, may God grant that your cognitive status awareness and the task of "building up yourselves on your most holy faith" (Jude 1:20, KJV) meet with the "peace which transcends all understanding" (Phil. 4:7, NIV). "And if on some point you think differently that too God will make clear to you" (Phil. 3:15, NIV).

CHAPTER 1:
LIABLE PROMISES ACROSS THE BOARD

?1: *WHAT* IS A LIABLE PROMISE AS IT *RELATES* TO EVERYONE'S *DEFINITION*

THE WORDS THAT COUNT

After the fall of Adam, God has promised his offspring the unrelenting human conflict with Satan, (Gen, 3:15 KJV). Hence, humans that are created equal are not born into equality. Aside from being created equal, twins are born into a virtual equality. They will evidently grow up with unequal fortunes in life. Their talents may differ providentially promising a different talent outcome as invested, (Matt. 25:15-30 KJV). Exposed to the society at large, soon they will find out that there are those who make promises to them unfulfilled whose reputations are tarnished thereby. For example, bargaining, the Reubenites and the Gadites who preemptively define their promised land require Moses to insist, "but do what you have promised," to battle alongside the other ten tribes to define their promised allocations beyond the Jordan river, (Numbers 32:24, NIV). Then, there are those who have rejected promises meant to do them good who are stuck on ill-fortune forever. The ill-fortune bound usually are the disappointed persons who resolve or vow to discount or annul the word of another promisor, thereby perpetuating their life frustrations. Of course, those subjected to unfulfilled promises are hurt deeply with scares in purview of their Creator. It is conclusive that all people – great, small, in between –notably will relate and transact by words of promise that will affect each other. Words matter to the hearers positively or negatively. Consider the respective warnings of Moses and the Lord Jesus that relate to life, death, and idle words! "But I [Jesus] say unto you, that every idle word that men shall speak, they shall give account thereof in the day of judgment," (Matt 12:36 KJV).

He [Moses] said to them, 'Take to heart all the words I have solemnly declared to you this day, so that you may command your children to obey carefully all the words of this law. They are not just idle words for you--they are your life. By them you will live long in

the land you are crossing the Jordan to possess,'
(Deut. 32:46,47 NIV).

On the other hand, the current culture is dulled by idle words. Apparently, skeptics are prevailing a lot in the culture that trifles with the sketchy promissory in commercial advertisement, transactional warranties, political statements, technological solutions with much abandonment to the risk of idle words. The audience of the culturally accepted idle words has helplessly learned to discount or marginalize vital promissory as a safe way to cope with life. Therefore, it is certain that failures would supplant successes while discounting the words that count and the prevailing audience is grossly skeptical to all promises. Nevertheless, "in God we trust" statement by conviction remains the response of the faithful to the divine providence and promises, (see Figure 1:1).

Figure 1:1 FAITH TWO-LEGGED FAITH WALK IN EVIDENCE/HOPE

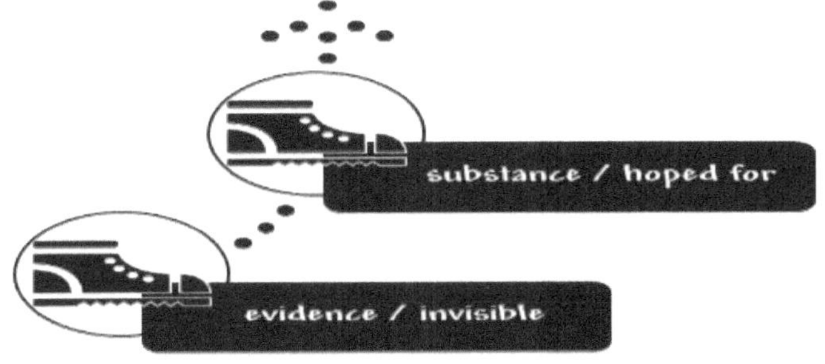

?2: *WHICH LIABLE PROMISE FACTOR IS REVIEWED* FOR *COMPREHENSION*

THE INTEGRITY OF THE PROMISOR

Whether skeptical or credulous, humans have been deceived like Eve or assured like Adam to yield to the tempting offers as in the garden of Eden. Some promises are very tangible, like foods to avoid in order that an individual can cope with certain chronic illnesses. Such diets need not go unnoticed or rejected to avoid bad consequences for life. On the other hand, some diet commercials over-promise health improvement too good to be true and worth ignoring. In the culture that has allowed many free offers riddled with hidden strings attached, offerees are weary to determine offers which are too good to be true with no strings attached. The integrity of the offeror or promisor takes precedence in reviewing a valid promise or offer worth the confidence or faith of the offerees. To reject or discount a valid promise brings a lifetime regret whether one is skeptical to the offer or credulous to a distracting offer. Studying the account in (2 Kings 7:1-2, 20, KJV), a close confidant of a king rejects or discounts the words of Elisha for abundant flour and barley supplies to bring an abrupt end to the ongoing famine the following day. The king's confidant sees the promissory come to pass but dies under the stampede of fellow citizens reaching out for the abundant supplies. The king's confidant has had a worldview that ridicules and limits God by saying, "if the LORD make windows in heaven, might these things be?" There is such a leaning on a personal understanding that must be put aside for the assurance necessary to take God at His word. Stakeholders must determine or review that which is valid from the presenting promises after having been assured of the *integrity* of *the promisor* – (In regard to God, believing that He **IS** faithful and truthful and that He is the **REWARDER** of seekers - see Figure 1:2).

Figure 1:2; GOD'S INTEGRITY DICTATES TO BLESS OR CURSE AS PROMISED

?3: *WHEN IS A LIABLE PROMISE FAITH RESOLVED BY APPLICATION*

AT THE BRINK OF RUIN

Endowered by the Creator, when God speaks truth to faith, faith comes by hearing His word, full of promises, either conditional or unconditional. It is within the fallen humanity to resolve first who to believe, then what to believe without discounting the promisor's word and come to a lifetime failure. Following the spiritual fall of Adam and Eve, Abel's sacrifice by faith pleases God. But very jealous, Cain resolves to kill Abel despite God's personal admonishment to Cain to watch out as "sin lieth at the door," (Genesis 4:7, KJV). In the aftermath of discounting God's word, the spiritual death scourging of Adam/Eve becomes apparent in the physical death of Abel but with a marker: the speaking blood of Abel. "From the blood of Abel unto the blood of Zacharias, which perished between the altar and the temple, verily I say unto you, it shall be required of this generation" expounds our Lord, Jesus Christ, (Luke 11.51, KJV). Later Christ hears some of them, during His trial with Pilate, say, "His blood be on us, and on our children," (Matthew 27:25, KJV). Also, the blood money, 30 pieces of Silver, paid to betray Him secures the potter's field to bury foreigners, (Matthew 27:8 KJV). However, given the irony of the speaking blood, forgiveness is freely offered to that generation, and all mankind, through "Jesus the Mediator of the new covenant, and through the blood of sprinkling that speaks better things than that of Abel," (Hebrews 12:24, NKJV). The blood of Jesus speaks to faith in His Mediation for the forgiveness of sins to those who believe. Such believers are saved by grace through faith original to Christ. Such faith marks a new beginning, birth of a new creation for the individual. Such faith must be kept as the forensic evidence to make expectations real for those things also freely given in Christ. Such faith in repeat response to His promises is necessary when walking with God to please Him. When God is pleased with such an agent of faith, He promises to grant the heart's desire of the believer. Of course, there are many other persuasions toward achieving people's heart desires. Sure, Adam and Eve are given the wide range of choices inclusive of many fruits for pleasure with the narrow exception of the only one fruit that kills. Yet by choice, they go astray through the only one way, consuming the one killer fruit. Conversely, only one way is being offered back into eternal life, although many ways are being taken into the eternal human jeopardy. The one-way inverse is profound. Christ is given exclusively for salvation by faith and inclusively to resolve life issues according to God's providence and promises proportionate to the faith walk in a lifestyle (see

Figure 1:1). In the neglect of God's promises that require faith, Evangelical Spiritual formation atrophies fast. Blessed are those who have learned to taste and see that the Lord is good to value His promissory interventions in human   affairs.

?4: *WHY* IS A LIABLE PROMISE FIDELITY *DIFFERENTIATED* IN *ANALYSIS*

FOR THE LOST PERCEPTIVE OR DISSONANCE

Among some Evangelical startups, the humanistic faith certainly breeds a lifelong failure if it goes on unchecked during the intervening crisis of life common to man. To avoid being riddled with doubts at the point of some disappointments in life, Paul primarily avoids in his messages the usage of the "persuasive wisdom of men" so that he cultivates no disciple with a faith resting on a carnal channel, (1 Corinthians 2:4, KJV). Some preachers may also exercise due diligence to differentiate from persuasive packages when engaging the pulpit. Rather they are to deliver the word of Christ characterized as "spirit and life" in feeding the laity that may not live by bread alone but by every word of God to cultivate Spiritual formative faith intake of the hearer. Secondarily, Paul warns the exposed Evangelicals like the Galatians whose spiritual faith is being subjected to carnal persuasion not to get bewitched and obscure the life-long Spiritual evidence. He asks, "Are ye so foolish? having begun in the Spirit, are ye now made perfect by the flesh?" (Galatians 3;1-3, KJV). So, it also goes with the task of the preachers to mitigate the Galatian-like vulnerability among the Evangelicals that must care.

Unlike some pastors, our Lord mitigates with warnings and prayer for Peter's faith that is perceived to fail when challenged to deny Him. It has become the current prevailing trial of our time to err in words and deeds. The cock is crowing, let every disciple self-examine to put an end to the besetting carnal absurdity. Christ has turned around to behold Peter and all the carnally minded as if to reinforce his statement, "blessed is he, whosoever shall not be offended in me," (Matthew 11:6, KJV). The PEW researchers, beside the LORD, need not continue to uncover the behavioral failure that goes on among some Evangelicals apparently due to some of the just who forego the Spiritual faith in their walk.

?5: *WHERE* IS A LIABLE PROMISE *ACCOUNTING* FOR TRUST THROUGH *SYNTHESIS*

IN A REGRESSIVE STATE

Peter walks on water toward our Lord who has asked him to proceed toward Him on water. Soon, he goes down drowning as the storm intensifies. Then he calls on the Lord to save him. The Lord reaches out swiftly to Him to prevent the accident while He asks, "O thou of little faith, wherefore didst thou doubt," (Matthew 14:30-31, KJV)? Peter does not give up on the Lord who saves but discounts the very promise in situ and dulls the assurance of a steady walk on water despite the evidence of the real Jesus still afloat on waters. The sights of the strong waves have promised disaster that overrides Peter's walk by faith in the promise of Jesus. After the episode, the rest of the disciples retain just the lifetime memory of failing to walk on waters with the Lord Jesus at the opportune time. Momentarily, borne on the waters, He has shared a divine status with the humbled Peter who walks back on water with Him to join the other disciples to worship the perceived Son of God in the tranquil of their boat, (Matthew 14:33, KJV). Later, as Peter recalls the past glorious moment with Christ, he sobs deeply and personally where the cock crows. And how the Lord has prayed that Peter's faith will not fail for a lifetime. Supposing Peter has excused his denial as the inevitable by accounting that Satan's desire of him and Jesus' prayer for him are to blame. Rather Peter sobs after Christ who restores His own to the level more than that of the evil conqueror. The after-effect of Peter's denial is his sacred responsibility to strengthen and feed the Lord's sheep and lambs. Peter has learned to feed them not by bread alone but with God's word, given the growth factor in the "sincere milk of the word," (1 Peter 2:2, KJV) who are "nourished up in the words of faith and of good doctrine" (1 Timothy 4:6, KJV).

?6: *WHOSE LIABLE PROMISE PARTNER IS VENERATED BY EVALUATION*

THE DIVINE ADORATION

Walking by faith in God is appraised in the worshiping of God in spirit and truth. It takes a stepwise faith to please God and not to be untruthful in praising Him or perpetuating cultural arrogance. The Scripture says two cannot walk together if they do not agree. The promise of God solicits consent and conviction as entailed in the promise. As God and His faith agent walk together in His surround, good report and worship are bound to prevail. The evidence is replete in the epistles to the Hebrews for our stepwise instruction on faith presenting the exemplars who have obtained good reports. Peter has emphasized that Christians can partake in God's divine nature through faith in His great and precious promises, (1 Peter 2:4, KJV). In Galatian 2:20, Paul testifies that his lifestyle is invigorated by the faith of the Son of God, not having his own righteousness (Philippians 3:9,15, KJV). Hence the humbled Evangelical is being enabled to be holy as He is Holy. Let the primary concern of the Evangelicals shift from the cultivating of good reports to the monitoring of their trust in God as the precursor to their accruable good reports by benefits. The Holy Spirit warns that in the later times, some will do away with the faith worldview (1 Timothy 4:1, KJV). In Luke 18:8, it is also the concern of Christ that when He returns faith may be absent from the various apparent Christian lifestyles. His own has lacked faith in Him the first time coming, notwithstanding His triumph. The second time, His church persons may end up lacking the demonstrative faith in His person current to their lifestyle. May it never be so, I pray. Christ is not only the way or the truth but life up-to-the-minute. Also, it must be remembered that Christ, as the author and finisher, measures faith: the great, the little, and the void. The Churches in the East, West or worldwide awaits Christ's return by faith to see Him and be like Him as promised. Recollecting, the first advent of Christ has on record the faith-failure of His own people. Not again, but the born-again persons, another brand of His own people seem careless in perpetuating a promissory-discounting with a faith-lacking lifestyle prior His second advent.

CHAPTER 2:
LIABLE PROMISES CULTIVATE JACOB'S STEPWISE FAITH

?1: *WHAT* IS A LIABLE PROMISE AS IT *RELATES* TO JACOB

BIRTHRIGHT, FROM BETHEL TO HARAN

Humans are created equal but not born with equal opportunities even in a royal family. As earlier stated, aside from being created equal, twins are born with the same factors but often are growing-up with the unequal fortunes in life. The claims of the skeptics fall flat given Jacob's life for a reference. Esau has the birthright promise but discounted and exchanged it for food with a lifetime failure. Esau's twin brother, Jacob is a nonstarter until age forty with a lifetime success for counting on the promissory of a birthright, spiritually speaking.

Esau cooks better, given that his blind father, Isaac, longs for his savory dish. Self-reliant Esau is hairy built, a strong hunter as if his charisma is by the dictates of his birthright. While that promising birthright appeals to the stay-at-home Jacob, Jacob's modest dish appeals to the hungry Esau who is an accomplished cook. Then Jacob steps up his cooking skill, his mother assisting, to satisfy the appetite of his father, and to receive the blessings of the birthright. Consequently, Jacob escapes into the wilderness to avoid being killed by an angry and supplanted Esau. But, unlike Esau, Jacob is unmarried, afraid for his life, and on the run alone with an intangible birthright. The escape route extends about 600 unfamiliar kilometers in the wild, from Beersheba to Haran. Jacob realizes his vulnerability to hunger and death, given the sojourning days ahead with his meager supplies.

Figure 2:1 NORTH DISTRICT, YIZRE'EL, WITH THE RUGGED ANTIQUITY, 2017

Weary Jacob takes a nap dreaming, and the promissory God shows up in the dream. God promises him of the future afar and near in the dream saying,

I am the LORD, the God of your father Abraham and the God of Isaac; the land on which you lie, I will give it to you and to your descendants. 'Your descendants will also be like the dust of the earth, and you will spread out to the west and to the east and to the north and to the south; and in you and in your descendants shall all the families of the earth be blessed. Behold, I am with you and will keep you wherever you go and will bring you back to this land; for I will not leave you until I have done what I have promised you,' (Genesis 28:13-15, NASV).

Jacob wakes up impressed with an invisible God and makes a vow by faith saying, "If God will be with me and will keep me on this journey that I take and will give me food to eat and garments to wear, and I return to my father's house in safety, then the LORD will be my God," (Genesis 28:20-21, NASV). Note that the upkeep promises of God to Jacob has become the assurance of what Jacob is hoping for along with the evidence of the personally felt presence of the invisible God. **Faith as defined in Hebrews 11:1 is initiated in the life of Jacob and leveraged by a divine promise for a journey with God to become of God: The God of Jacob.**

Esau remains well supplied with wives, children as chiefs that the traded birthright remains elusive, materially speaking. Centuries later, his progenitors are the Edomites, ahead of the Israelites to form a formidable kingdom while the descendants of Jacob roam the wilderness with the God of Jacob to the promised land to form the Israeli kingdom. Nevertheless, Esau suffers a lifetime failure, Jacob gains a lifetime success. By a spiritual measure, a man's life does not consist in the abundance of his possession so states Jesus Christ two millennia later. Jesus is aware of the opulent Herod the Great dynasty, the descendants of Esau who progressively supplant the regency rights of the descendants of Jacob during the time of the gospel in Israel. The promises of God solicit faith that engages His evidential companionship for all realities temporal or eternal to cultivate the faith agent, in crisis, as of God for God

?2: *WHICH LIABLE PROMISE FACTOR IS REVIEWED* FOR JACOB

DIVINE CONFIRMATION FOR HIS HOME GOING

Jacob testifies of his honest life for 20 years in Haran. Laban, his uncle, and father-in-law, perceives and shares from God's favor to Jacob who is comfortable and exceedingly prosperous with a large family. All the while, Jacob's helpful mother is dead and buried, his blind father lives on and the faithful God waits on him for his safe return-trip to Bethel as promised. **A start-up faith need go on stepwise, for a walk with the promissory God who is always reviewing the intrinsic faith.**

The inimical frown of Laban clannish envy is at a crisis level for immigrant Jacob to handle. Jacob's unarmed large convoy escape trip home to face the revengeful Esau makes the flashback ominous for Jacob to bear. Then the God of all comfort takes a promise to Jacob's faith saying, "Return to the land of your fathers and to your relatives, and I will be with you," (Genesis 31:3, NAS).

Laban is capable to crush Jacob who is on the run, pursued and overtaken. The Almighty God makes the enmity of Laban to be at peace with the timidity of Jacob. Laban challenges Jacob saying "Now you have done foolishly. It is in my power to do you harm, but the God of your father spoke to me last night, saying, 'Be careful not to speak either good or bad to Jacob,'" (Genesis 31:28b-29, NAS).   Fears that deplete faith cause foolishness to discount the protective promise of God or assume His non-existence.

Laban is respecting Jacob's invisible God's warning to allow Jacob's decision to return to Canaan unhindered. Despite his personal encounter with God, Laban's faith remains on the missing idol for his worship. Jacob is accused of abducting the missing idol. Rachel hides the idol undetected during Laban's search while Jacob claims his vindication. God does not condone idolatry but does await the repentance of His own sinning meanwhile in His longsuffering by His Integrity. Rachel's hidden idolatry spreads in the camp of Jacob openly for Jacob to realize and disapprove the practice at Shechem. The promise of God is not just a prediction for fulfillment but an active grooming of the faith agent to review his or her standing with Him.

Figure 2:2 DAVID RIVER, YIZRE'EL, WITH RUGGED ANTIQUITY, 2017

?3: *WHEN* IS A LIABLE PROMISE FAITH *RESOLVED* BY JACOB

WRESTLING WITH GOD

As Laban departs, Jacob reviews his faith in relation to God and concern for survival. He knows his limitation going forward to meet with Esau's camp more formidable than Laban's. God makes His Angels walk pass Jacob on his way casually and visibly. At the place named *Mahanaim*, the visible Angelic camp is suggestive that Jacob's camp is fortified beyond his imagination (Genesis 32:1-2, NAS).

Jacob brings his fear of Esau to God and pleads in a prayer of faith over both the temporary and eternal dimension of God's promise. It is to be understood that faith which makes God a companion to His servant who is unworthy of His grace, regardless of past successes must be reapplied unto victory in the ensuing struggles of life:

> O God of my father Abraham and God of my father Isaac, O LORD, who said to me, 'Return to your country and to your relatives, and I will prosper

you,' I am unworthy of all the lovingkindness and of all the faithfulness which You have shown to Your servant; for with my staff only I crossed this Jordan, and now I have become two companies. Deliver me, I pray, from the hand of my brother, from the hand of Esau; for I fear him, that he will come and attack me and the mothers with the children. For You said, 'I will surely prosper you and make your descendants as the sand of the sea, which is too great to be numbered,' (Genesis 32:9-12, NAS).

After the prayers, in a dream struggling, God engages with him and declares, "Your name shall no longer be Jacob, but Israel; for you have striven with God and with men and have prevailed." (Genesis 32:28, NAS). Eventually, Esau and Jacob meet, weeping over each other, with no clash but at peace with one another. They both are surprisingly affluent enough respectively to disregard the concern for a birthright. Jacob's family watch Jacob insists on appeasing Esau with

two hundred female goats and

twenty male goats,

two hundred ewes and

twenty rams,

thirty milking camels and their colts,

forty cows and

ten bulls,

twenty female donkeys and

ten male donkeys.) gifts for Esau, (Genesis 32:14-15, NAS).

Nevertheless, Jacob remains suspicious or rationalizing and settles at Shechem, short of Bethel, not as a stopover but his indefinite settlement in Canaan contrary to the clear instruction of his God to dwell in Bethel. When fear persists, the need for one's authored faith intensifies to resolve it by the endurance of faith while pressing forward.

?4: *WHY* IS A LIABLE PROMISE FIDELITY *DIFFERENTIATED* IN JACOB

INSISTING ON BETHEL FOR ABODE

Shechem is about 50 kilometers short of the trip to Bethel, being the proper destination of the round trip to Haran twenty-two years ago, where the faith of Jacob in the promise of God has been animated. Notwithstanding the discounting of his own vow and divine promissory, Jacob feels safe to buy a land to settle his residence and an alter for God in Shechem. This is a classic wandering from faith by a faith-agent being schooled. To walk together with God, there must be an agreement and avoidance to lean on one's self understanding but God, (Proverbs 3:5, KJV).

At Shechem, Jacob's only teenage daughter is raped. Joseph, the immediate younger brother of the rapped observes the horror of the sexual immorality and agony that grip the entire house of Jacob. Other siblings arrange a normalization by inter-marriage and restitution by circumcision of all men of Shechem. The ordinance of circumcision is abused for a mass murder revenge of all the men and plunder of Shechem by Simeon and Levi, the sons of Jacob. In addition, the worship of idols festers in the family and Jacob knows about it (the ten commandments by Moses is written 400 years later). God is not pleased, and His longsuffering is not in question. Now Jacob is scared and vulnerable to the attack of the Canaanites and the Perizzites redressing the social injustice in Shechem.

"Then God said to Jacob, 'Arise, go up to Bethel and live there, and make an altar there to God, who appeared to you when you fled from your brother Esau.'" (Genesis 35:1, NASB). It is for Jacob to believe and abide in the only true God at Bethel. Jacob renews allegiance to God and no idol or paganistic figurine is allowed in the final trip. Then the invisible surround terror of God comes along to frighten foes as Jacob's camp moves to Bethel where God affirms His promise and blessings to Jacob. The faith of Jacob at this point is certified with Divine pleasure over him being self-appraised and listed in the annals of the heroes of faith (Hebrews 11:20-21, KJV). Unashamed of Jacob in (Genesis 35:9-13, NASB):

> Then God appeared to Jacob again when he came
> from Paddan-aram, and He blessed him.
> God said to him,
> 'Your name is Jacob,
> You shall no longer be called Jacob,
> But Israel shall be your name.'

Thus, He called him Israel.
God also said to him,
'I am God Almighty,
Be fruitful and multiply,
A nation and a company of nations shall come from you,
And kings shall come forth from you.
The land which I gave to Abraham and Isaac,
I will give it to you, And I will give the land to your descendants after you,' (Genesis 35:9-13, NASB).

God has clearly instructed resisting Jacob to dwell or abide in Bethel. While resisting, multiple misfortunes prevail in the camp. Deborah, Rachel's nurse, dies, and she is buried below Bethel under the oak. Jacob's family hurries a departure to Beersheba. Unfortunately, Rachel dies while on the way during childbirth, close to the town of Bethlehem shortly before arriving at Beersheba. Lingering at Shechem has its delayed effect. Reflecting at Beersheba, Rachael, his beloved wife, and Rebekah, his enabling mother, have passed away respectively. Jacob's first son, Simeon, rapes Bilhah, the servant of Rachael and 4th wife of Jacob to another dismay of the impressionable Joseph with a memory to serve him good later when fleeing the seduction of Potiphar. In the final days of the blind Isaac, Esau and Jacob take care of the

Patron Isaac and his burial ceremony at Hebron which is situated between Shechem and Beersheba. Sometimes later, Jacob relocates to Hebron where he buries Leah and expects himself to be buried in Hebron notwithstanding his sojourn in Egypt eventually. Indeed, faith and reasoning do clash to precipitate and explain some of the misfortunes of life, but the differentiation lies in the faith-agent holding on to a faithful God by his promise and avoid leaning on a personal understanding.

?5: *WHERE* IS A LIABLE PROMISE *ACCOUNTING* FOR TRUST THROUGH JACOB'S STRUGGLE

LEAVING THE PROMISED LAND FOR EGYPT

The entire Canaan land is crowding up because Esau and Jacob respective territories have been expanding. It is significant that for grazing expansion, Jacobs' family will wander north beyond Shechem where Joseph locates his brothers and begins his enslavement. Esau relocates his camp to the hill country of Seir. Riches may increase, the faith agent's realities are bound in God Himself. Esau is not a faith agent, but Jacob is the one who is at a certain spiritual development stage. Eventually, Jacob relocates to Egypt as famine ravages the land of Canaan to refresh him spiritually.

For 17 years Jacob sorrows over the absence of his son, Joseph, presumed dead but sold into slavery in Egypt. Joseph enjoys God's presence and elevation to the high executive position to help his father and siblings in due time. With famine on the rise Jacob's household make two trips to Egypt and discover the rise of Joseph as the divine provision for their survival. By the first trip, the stars (his brothers) have made their bow to Joseph. By the second trip, apparently the Sun and Moon (Jacob and Leah) bow to the request for Benjamin by Joseph. Leah is presumed dead before the relocation to Egypt. Joseph and Pharaoh instruct Jacob and family to relocate to Egypt from Hebron. Jacob is eager to see Joseph and die. Jacob with his birthright now prays for his death right.

So, Israel set out with all that he had, and came to Beersheba, and offered sacrifices to the God of his father Isaac. God spoke to Israel in visions of the night and said, 'Jacob, Jacob.' And he said, 'Here I am.' He said, 'I am God, the God of your father; do not be afraid to go down to Egypt, for I will make you a great nation there. I will go down with you to Egypt, and I will also surely bring you up again; and Joseph will close your eyes,' (Genesis 46:2-4, NAS).

God wants to be called the God of Jacob along with God of Isaac and God of Abraham. Jacob's faith must bear the full accounting that God is his substance. To leave Beersheba for the South seems to present a flashback. Jacob consults with God by sacrifice. This is the last recorded personal didactic faith encounter of Jacob with God. God's presence and promise are assured to Jacob even in relocating to Egypt. Joseph's fortune in Egypt becomes the evidence of the Invisible God at work. Jacob leaves Beersheba behind as the agent of promise by faith to birth a great nation of Israel within the nation of Egypt.

?6: *WHOSE LIABLE PROMISE PARTNER IS VENERATED* BY JACOB

GOD OF JACOB IN ESSENCE GLORIFIED

God of Jacob embarking on Jacob's royal entourage has Judah in the forefront as the dispatch rider to Goshen. Joseph comes to Goshen to welcome his father with the invitation to visit with Pharaoh. The land of Egypt has been offered freely with no strings attached. Jacob is now the agent of God in reconciliation to the blessing of God. Pharaoh's palace presents the impression of affluence that can challenge the materialist at heart. Jacob struggles with Pharaoh's interview but blesses him, like the King of the Jews before Pilate centuries later. Notwithstanding his apology for his past sorrowful years and low achievement compared to his predecessor, Jacob keeps on blessing Pharaoh.

> And Jacob blessed Pharaoh. Pharaoh said to Jacob, 'How many years have you lived?' So, Jacob said to Pharaoh, 'The years of my sojourning are one hundred and thirty; few and unpleasant have been the years of my life, nor have they attained the

years that my fathers lived during the days of their sojourning.' And Jacob blessed Pharaoh and went out from his presence, (Genesis 47:7b-10, NASB).

Jacob is confident that God is his and he is God's for the next 17 years in the Egyptian comfort. It is as if God refreshes him for 17 years in repeat of the time span earlier spent with Joseph growing up. Perhaps it is also to redress his self-appraising of his passed ordeal before Pharaoh. He has testified,

> The years of my sojourning are one hundred and thirty; few and unpleasant have been the years of my life, nor have they attained the years that my fathers lived during the days of their sojourning, (Genesis 47:9, NASB).

At age 147 years, it feels satisfying for Jacob to prepare for his death with ample blessings for each of his children. He grafts the two sons of Joseph into the ranks of the original twelve. Isaac's blessing is narrowed to one. In contrast, Jacob blesses Joseph, his sons Ephraim and Manase, and his 11 siblings making it fourteenfold blessings with eternal consequences. With no alter in situ, Jacob blesses and bows in worship to his Divine companion, "the God who has been my shepherd all my life to this day, the angel who has redeemed me from all evil" (Genesis 48:15-16, NASB)

When the time for Israel to die drew near, he called his son Joseph and said   to him, 'Please, if I have found favor in your sight, place now your hand under my thigh and deal with me in kindness and faithfulness. Please do not bury me in Egypt, but when I lie down with my fathers, you shall carry me out of Egypt and bury me in their burial place.' And he said, 'I will do as you have said.' He said, 'Swear to me.' So, he swore to him. Then Israel bows in worship at the head of the bed before expiring, (Genesis 47:29-31, NAS).

From birthright to death-right, the LORD has tent-schooled Jacob in his pilgrimage to be an agent of faith by promise, in tandem becoming the agent of promise by faith, that has graduated into the principal of faith with the benefit of a good report. "By faith Jacob, as he was dying, blessed each of the sons of Joseph, and worshiped, leaning on the top of his staff," (Hebrews 11:21, KJV). Considering the Law as a school master inaugurated about 450 years after Jacob's lifetime to be useful in evaluating his odyssey as follows: as touching the 10th commandment, the covetousness of Esau's birthright is also an idolatry (Colossians 3:5, KJV). But God redeemed him not to have any other God other than Himself. As touching the 1st to the 9th Commandments, his biblical record is free from infringing any of them during his 70 years of pilgrimage as an agent or student of faith. Jacob acknowledges that God has redeemed him (Genesis 48:15-16, NASB). The Law as a school master teaches redemption from aberration through a lamb sacrifice, foreshadowing Jesus as the redemptive lamb endearing to faith unto salvation. God's promise has been effectual within and beyond the lifetime of Jacob's enduring faith. God's promise frontloads all of Jacob's needs - natural and supernatural, material wise and spiritual - challenging Jacob's stepwise walk by faith. Jacob's faith benefits have included his GOOD REPORT according to Hebrew chapter 11 discourse.

In preparing to walk by faith, it is noteworthy that Jacob's faith, in a stepwise discipline, corresponds to the Western classic Bloom's Cognitive Taxonomy six levels of self-questioning by default at each stage of his spiritual formation. Coincidentally, each stage receives an answer to the futuristic Aaronic composite prayer on Israel prescribed in (Num. 6:24-26, KJV) also annotated along briefly:

1, **Definition**: *What* is needed for his survival? Jacob departs to Haran and he *relates* to God's promise of companionship by faith, (Gen. 28:13-14, KJV). *God blesses Israel* (Num. 6:24a, KJV).

2, **Comprehension**: *Which* state of affair is preferred? Jacob leaves Haran and he *reviews* God's promise for approval by faith, (Gen. 28:15; 31:3, KJV). *God keeps Israel* (Num. 6:24b, KJV),

3, **Application**: *When* is his fear assailing? Jacob is afraid of meeting with Esau and he *resolves* his fear by faith in God's promise to do him good, having changed his name to Israel (Gen. 32:12,28, KJV). *God shines His face on Israel* (Num. 6:25a. KJV).

4, **Analysis**: *Why* is he conflicted? Jacob is conflicted at Shechem and he *differentiates* Bethel as the true destination by faith in God's promise, (Gen. 35:1–2, KJV) (Hebrews 11:20–21, KJV). More of Jacob's faith is discussed in the context of the Hebraic exemplars in the Hebrews epistle. *God is gracious to Israel* (Num. 6:25b, KJV).

5, **Synthesis**: *Where* goes his future? Jacob feels adrift going to Egypt and he *accounts* for assurance by faith in God's promise and directives before embarking on the trip, (Gen 46:2–4, KJV). *God lifts His countenance upon Israel* (Num. 6:26a, KJV).

6, **Evaluation**: *Whose* is the glory? God is unashamed of Jacob. Jacob *appraises* his life by God's faithfulness to His promises, and he worships the "God of Jacob" while blessings his successors through faith, (Gen. 48:15–16, KJV). Jacob has obtained good report. He has walked and matured by faith that pleases God. God has been in the pilgrimage with Jacob by His word of promise to make Jacob, as in (2 Peter 1:4, KJV) partake of His divine nature by promise abiding. Hence the benefit of faith in the liable promises of God is a good report, an evangelic life, (Hebrews 11:2,39-40, KJV). *God gives peace to Israel* (Num. 6:26b, KJV).

THE MORALS OF FAITH IN GOD'S PROMISES

A: In every condition of a Christian life, Divine Promissory solicits a quickening faith through the promisee' evidence of the invisible in binary to the assurance of the expected and tries an enduring faith of the promisee integral to obtaining a good report as a Divine associate (See A: 1, 2, 3, 4 & 5 below).

B: In corollary to A: above, an apparent faith is stifled or dead, if it is depleted of a working evidence. And an apparent working evidence is marginalized, displeasing to God, if it is depleted of faith (See B: 1, 2 below).

A: The Teachings from the Scriptures:
1, For all the promises of God in Him (Christ) are yea, and in Him Amen, unto the glory of God by us, (2 Corinthians 1:20, KJV). Now faith is the substance of things hoped for,

the evidence of things not seen. For by it the elders obtained a good report, (Hebrews 11:1-2, KJV).

2. Whereby are given unto us exceeding great and precious promises: that by these ye might be partakers of the divine nature, having escaped the corruption that is in the world through lust, (2 Peter 1:4, KJV).

3, I have been crucified with Christ; it is no longer I who live, but Christ lives in me; and the life which I now live in the flesh I live by faith in the Son of God, who loved me and gave Himself for me, (Galatians 2:20 NKJV).

4, That the trial of your faith, being much more precious than of gold that perisheth, though it be tried with fire, might be found unto praise and honor and glory at the appearing of Jesus Christ, (1 Peter 1:7, KJV).

5, Therefore we also, since we are surrounded by so great a cloud of witnesses, let us lay aside every weight, and the sin which so easily ensnares us, and let us run with endurance the race that is set before us, looking unto Jesus, the author and finisher of our faith, who for the joy that was set before Him endured the cross, despising the shame, and has sat down at the right hand of the throne of God, (Hebrews 12:1-2, NKJV).

B: The Didactic Corollary from the Scriptures
1, Seest thou how faith wrought with his works, and by works was faith made perfect, (James 2:22, KJV)? Being

confident of this very thing, that he which hath begun a good work in you will perform it until the day of Jesus Christ, (Philippians 1:6, KJV).

2, But without faith it is impossible to please Him, for he who comes to God must believe that He is, and that He is a rewarder of those who diligently seek Him. (Hebrews 11:6, KJV). Then they said to Him, "What shall we do, that we may work the works of God?" Jesus answered and said to them, "This is the work of God, that you believe in Him whom He sent," (John 6:28-29, NKJV). Many will say to me in that day, Lord, Lord, have we not prophesied in thy name? and in thy name have cast out devils? and in thy name done many wonderful works? And then will I profess unto them, I never knew you: depart from me, ye that work iniquity, (Matthew 7:22-23, KJV).

Chapter three provides the result of the investigation that ascertains the instructional presentation of the life of faith in a stepwise model exemplified and paralleled to the Western Instructional designs from the Epistles to the Hebrews.

CHAPTER 3:
LIABLE PROMISES EXEMPLARS' FAITH IN A RESEARCH STUDY

COGNITIVE EXPLORATION OF THE DISCOURSE (HEBREWS 11– 12:2, KJV)

This section, taken from the author's academic study, explores the background data collectable on the exemplars while positioning the divine promissory as a strategic variable and an enabler of faith with the benefit of a good report. "All these people were still living by faith when they died" (Hebrews 11:13). The tactical variable is faith as the means for their venture. The Epistle to the Hebrews narratives presents some chiastic structures, in parts or whole, reflecting the western cognitive didactic objectives as to its instructional design.

Just as the Hebraic acrostic and Hellenic chiastic arrangements in scripture may differ by cultural literary styles, they approximate cognition to the core message. Considering the Hebraic didactics of Psalms 36-37, prior the Hellenistic era, Dr. Benun explains that "we find a chiastic structure based on the number of acrostic letters in each section."[1] Similarly one may infer a universal cognitive process for all learners, whether Oriental, Hellenistic, Western - literate or illiterate. "Most scholars analyze the Epistle to the Hebrews from only a Western linear approach. Other Scholars like Vanhoye, Neeley, G.H. Gutherie, and Gerlardindi have suggested a chiastic perspective."[2] So early chiastic analysis tends to suppress the unity of the expository and the hortatory sections in the Hebraic discourse.[3] "A survey of literature on chiasm indicates, however, that the use of the word "chiasm" is not limited to the parallelism of words or phrases; it is also used to refer to inversion of ideas or

---

[1] Ronald Benun. *"Evil and the Disruption of Order a Structural Analysis of the Acrostics in the First Book of Psalms"* 2017. http://www.jhsonline.org/cocoon/JHS/a055.html Accessed November 20, 2017.

[2] David Mark Health. "Chiastic Structures in Hebrews: A Study of Form and Function in Biblical Discourse" *Dissertation presented for the Degree of Doctor of Philosophy in Biblical Languages at the University of Stellenbosch South Africa* (March 2011), Abstract.

[3] Gareth Lee Cockerill. *The International Commentary on the New Testament: The Epistle to the Hebrews.* (Grand Rapids: Wm. B. Eerdmans Publication, 2012), 61.

concepts in a broad sense."[4] Perceptively, the chiastic concept motif of the entire Epistle to the Hebrews point to a study variable, such as "promise" in the data collection applied to this investigation. And there is a chiastic perspective of Hebrews Chapter 11 cognitive to clarify pedagogy on "faith" that corresponds with the classic Blooms Taxonomy, six levels[5], in the structure of the Western didactics. In respect to the study variable "promise" (Greek word: epaggellomai), consider the following quadruple [A, A' to D, D'] chiasm structure on promise in the entire Epistle to the Hebrews:

> A. PROMISEE's CRISIS of FEAR "Let us therefore fear, lest a promise" Hebrews 4:1 [KJV].
>
> B. PROMISEE's RESPONSE to FAITH "not slothful ... through faith ... inherit the promises" Hebrews 6:12 [KJV].
>
> C. PROMISEE's ENDURANCE of FAITH "after he had patiently endured, he

---

[4] Victor (Sung) Rhee "Chiasm and the Concept of Faith in Hebrews 11." *Bibliotheca Sacra* 327–45 (July–September 1998), 328.

[5] Blooms Taxonomy six levels: Knowledge, Comprehension, Application, Analysis, Synthesis, Evaluation. Reflecting on a concept - Knowledge level probes the [WHAT] in cognitive status, Comprehension level probes the [WHICH] in cognitive status, Applications level probes the [WHEN] in cognitive status, Analysis level probes the [WHY] in cognitive status, Synthesis level probes the [WHERE] in cognitive status, Evaluation probes the [WHOSE] in cognitive status. See Appendix B.

obtained the promise" Hebrews 6:15 [KJV].

D. PROMISOR of REPUTE "Wherein God ...shew unto the heirs of promise the immutability of His counsel" Hebrews 6:17 [KJV].

D'. PROMISOR of REPUTE worshipped by "tithes of Abraham, and blessed him that had the promises" Hebrews 7:6 [KJV]

C'. PROMISEE's ENDURANCE of FAITH "By faith he sojourned in the land of promise, as a stranger in a foreign country" Hebrews 11:9 [KJV].

B'. PROMISEE's RESPONSE to FAITH " All these people were still living by faith when they died. They did not receive the things promised" Hebrews 11:13 [KJV].

A'. PROMISEE's CRISIS of FEAR "He who had embraced the promises was about to sacrifice his one and only son" Hebrews 11:17 [KJV].

Apparently, correlating the preceding chiasm of the promissory to the classic Blooms Taxonomy, the chiasm [A, A' ... D, D'] begins in level 3 - [WHEN] or from the application level to level 6 – [WHOSE] or the evaluation level. Unaddressed are Blooms levels 1 and 2, or the "Knowledge level" – [WHAT] and the "Comprehension level"-[WHICH] of the promissory concept. Perhaps both levels have been deemed unchallenged cognitively or unrequired contextually. However, it is instructive to note that (A, A' or level 3) a divine promise by faith is applied [WHEN] in crisis; (B, B' or level 4) analyzed [WHY] for trust; monitored (C, C' or level 5) as enduring in directive [WHERE] to His will; evaluated (D, D' or level 6) to extol [WHOSE] divine reputation without discounting nor neglecting the worship of Him that over-rules. In review, section (D, D' or level 6) approximate the cognition of the promisee in trusting unflinchingly the Promisor of Repute for the conduct of Worship. It is the soliciting Divine Promissory that is adjuring the firm response by faith.

The faith narrations strategy of Hebrews chapter 11 passage (see figure 3.1a, 3.1b) is instructive in eliciting the instrumentality (dative) of faith in the conduct of the exemplars as the didactic motif for the imitator. Given the entire Epistle to the Hebrews "faith," as a term in the Greek, appears in the dative case 19 times; 18 in Hebrews chapter 11 alone and once in Hebrews chapter 4 verse 2. In Hebrews chapter 4, the usage of the word explicitly stages the dative case contextually, indicating that "not united by faith" is the *means* to the access failure into a divine rest and a disapproved lifestyle. Although there are about 27 shades of the dative case, in his book[6], *Greek Grammar Beyond the Basics*, Dr. Wallace, among other verses of scripture, illustrates the Dative of Means/Instrument of faith that accomplishes an action by referencing Hebrews 11:17. The verse shares a similar shade of the dative case in the chapter. Even the Genitive of Means is used in verses 6 and 33 to inform how faith takes effect. Semantically, "(t)he genitive of means seems to be, at times, slightly closer to a causal idea than the dative of means (the dat. is the normal case used to indicate means)."[7]   The Chiastic/Bloom's taxonomy structuring of Hebrews Chapter 11 turns the discourse into a metacognitive design, processing information for self-upgrading (by level / self-status awareness),[8] cognitive challenge with faith as the Means/Instrument for God's righteous ones who shall live out of faith (Hebrews 10:38-39), looking onto Jesus (Hebrews 12:1-2). The cognitive process or encounter of the promisee may be formally unaware of the Bloom's taxonomy while

---

[6] Daniel B. Wallace. *Greek Grammar: Beyond the Basics: An Exegetical Syntax of the New Testament* (Grand Rapids: Zondernvan, 1996), 163.

[7] Ibid., 125.

[8] Lori Anderson, et al. *A Taxonomy for Learning, Teaching, and Assessing: A Revision of Bloom's Taxonomy of Educational Objectives* (New York: Longman, 2001), 55. "*Metacognitive Knowledge* is knowledge about cognition in general as well as awareness of and knowledge about one's own cognition."

informally self-determining the (what, which, when, why, where, and whose) aspect of one's faith as the means. The following is the didactic-chiastic structure of Hebrews Chapter 11 with the cognitive terms underlined:

A, Hebrews 11:1-3, Faith is the means to _relating_ with immediacy to the world-visible and the word-invisible, [_WHAT_] [Blooms Level 1].

B, Hebrews 11:4-5, Faith is the means to _reviewing_ the victory of a fatal excellence and immortal translation, _[WHICH]_ [Blooms Level 2].

C, Hebrews 11:6-7, Faith is the means to _resolving_ the instance of "moved by fear," ((KJV) _[WHEN]_ [Blooms Level 3].

D, Hebrews 11:8-10, Faith is the means to _differentiating_ the effect of divine promissory while estranged, _[WHY]_ [Blooms Level 4].

E, Hebrews 11:11-12, Faith is the means to _accounting_ for resurrection of a post bearing womb, _[WHERE]_ [Blooms Level 5].

F, F', Hebrews 11: 13-16, Faith is the means to _appraising_ the supremacy of the divine prerogative and the unashamed, [_WHOSE_] [Blooms Level 6].

E', Hebrews 11:17–19, Faith is the means to _accounting_ for resurrection of a person of promise considered expiring, _[WHERE]_ [Blooms Level 5].

D', Hebrews 11:20–22, Faith is the means to _differentiating_ the effect of divine promissory while estranged, worshipping / blessing _[WHY]_ [Blooms Level 4].

C', Hebrews 11:23–31, Faith is the means to _resolving_ the instance of "fearing the wrath of a king," (KJV) _[WHEN]_ [Blooms Level 3].

B', Hebrews 11:32–38, Faith is the means to _reviewing_ the victory of the victor or victim of a mortal sword, _[WHICH]_ [Blooms Level 2].

A', Hebrews 11:39–40, Faith is the means to _relating_ with immediacy to the saints-present, past and future, [_WHAT_] [Blooms Level 1].

LIABLE PROMISES:

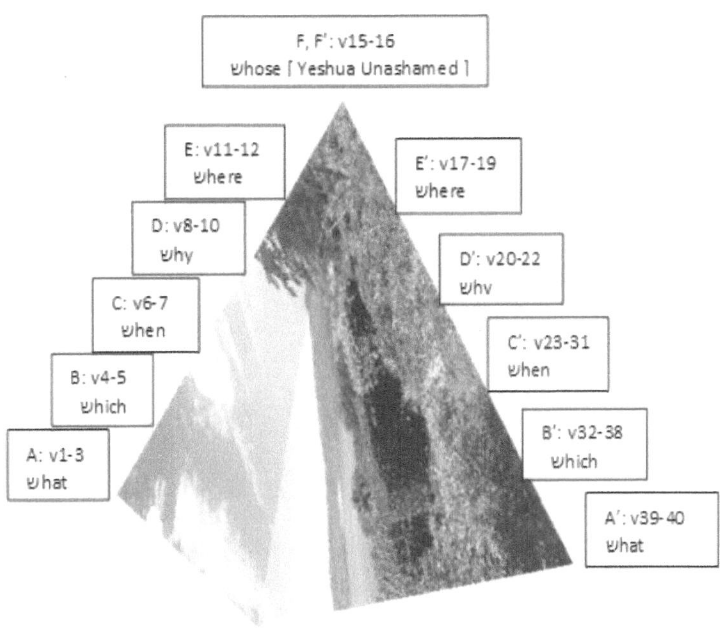

Figure 3:1a: CHIASM OF HEBREWS 11

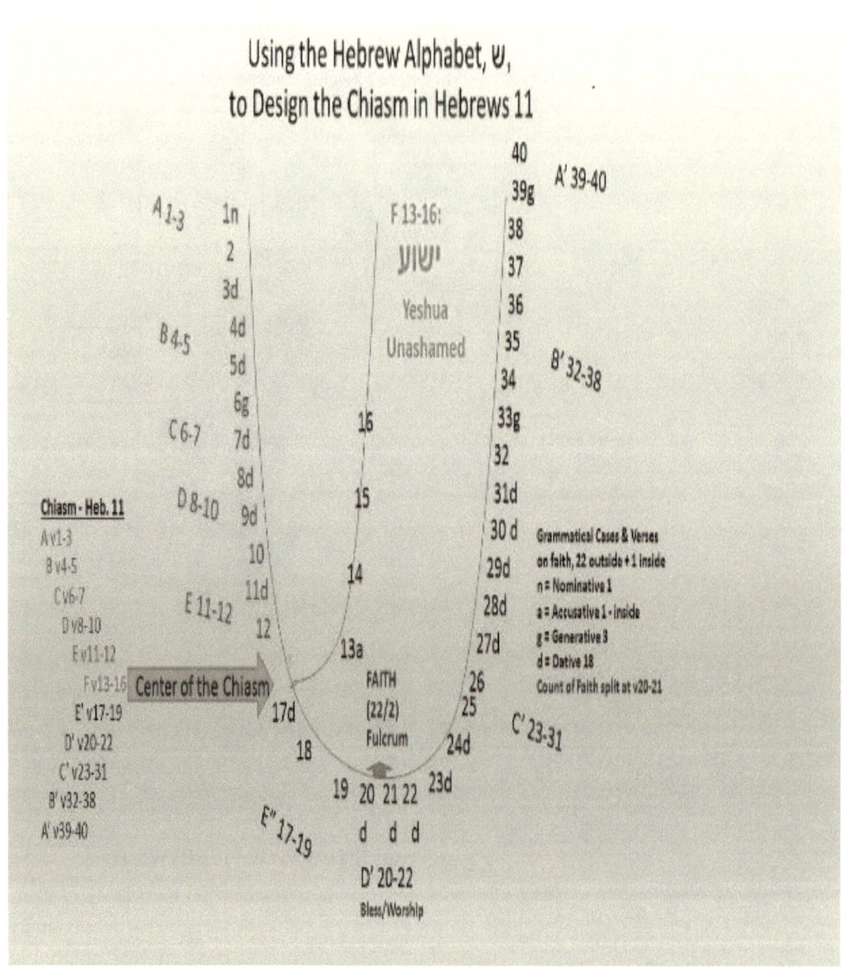

Figure 3.1b: CHIASM[9] OF HEBREWS 11

---

[9] Chiastic Structure −Like the Messianic Shin: see Gill Nuyten. "Secret of the Hebrew letter Shin" http://www.thelivingword.org.au/grand−design/session39.php accessed November 21, 2017

RESEARCH DATA SOURCING FROM THE BIBLE NARRATIVES ON THE EXEMPLARS

This section will bring together from the scriptural samples of incidence with annotations of the promissory contextual to the conviction and the afforded didactic threshold in the lives of the exemplars while doing the items scoring on the Likert scale. Regarding each variable, explicit claim or disclaim is determined from the expression of the subject or the biblical biographer. Implicit claim or disclaim is derived circumstantially by the biographer or the investigator. Indeterminant claim is assigned for lack of assurance or clarity. Please note that Isaac is a worthy exemplar but not data sampled for the purpose of the study by design. [See table 3:20 for the research variables applied to the research subjects or the biblical exemplars]

ABRAHAM

The writer of the Hebrews in chapter 11, inspires his readers with some instances of faith in Abraham's autobiography to give an instruction on the Christian race. Hebrews 11:8-10 discourse refreshes those that are baffled with the "WHY" of estrangement, which is core to their sojourning. Also, Hebrews 11:17-19 sites Abraham's faith in accounting for resurrection of the promised son at the brink of him sacrificing Isaac who has asked, "but WHERE is the lamb.?" (Genesis 22:7, KJV). Apparently, Abraham has become a stranger, trusting as promised under guidance. The promise in Genesis 12: 1-3 includes a land, a nation, a great name, and the boomerang of blessing or cursing from/to his acquaintances. Sojourning with God, the Promisor, eventually transcends the lifetime of Abraham. Within the promised land, he is bereaved:

> Abraham stood up from before his dead, and spake unto the sons of Heth, saying, I am a stranger and a sojourner with you: give me a possession of a burying place with you, that I may bury my dead out of my sight. (Genesis 23:3-4, KJV).

On the Likert Scale, given Hebrews 11, the following scores are assigned contextual to Genesis 12: pre-conduct 3, fearful 3, promise 5, faith 5, post-conduct 5; Genesis 22: pre-conduct 4, fearful 4, promise 5, faith 5, post-conduct 5; Genesis 23: pre-conduct 3, fearful 5, promise

5, faith 4, post-conduct 5. (See Appendix D data rows **abge12, abge22 and abge23**).

Annotation:

The Research Subject ID [1_Abraham] issues, crisis and narrative events variables:

1, Terah leaves UR of Chaldeans to Haran with his son Abram/Abraham. From Haran God with promises calls Abraham, 75 years old, to move to the land of promise, destination unknown (Genesis 12:1-3; Hebrews 11:8 KJV). Although father Terah has passed away, a current crisis or concern of Abraham and his pre-conduct are indeterminate. The claims that he receives a promise, and exercises faith with an exemplary conduct, are all explicit.

2, Abraham has with him as promised, the son Isaac whom he loves (Genesis 22:1-19; Hebrews 11:17-19 KJV). There is an implicit claim that his pre-conduct is nominal, and the testing presented to him is a crisis. He is asked to sacrifice the son on Mount Moriah, and he obeys trusting God to bring Isaac back to life. The claims that he holds unto a promise, and exercises faith with an exemplary conduct, are all explicit.

3, Abraham, 75 years old, travels with his wife Sarah, 65 years old to the land of promise. At the age of 127 years Sarah dies. And Isaac is 37 years old. All stay as immigrants in the land of promise. (Genesis 23:1-3;

Hebrews 11:9, KJV). Abraham's pre-conduct is indeterminate. The claim that he has faith is implicit. The claims of crisis, promise, while presenting an exemplary conduct, are all explicit.

SARAH

Sarah's faith is instructive in Hebrew 11:11-12 -WHERE- her faith accounts for a chronic barren womb to conceive with a child. With the delay (from age 65 to 89 years), she rationalizes and considers herself out of the loop to fulfilling the promise of a child to Abraham. The discounting of the promissory of God preys on that which is thought to be impossible. Then Sarah receives the direct promise: Genesis 18:14, "Is anything too hard for the LORD? At the time appointed I will return unto thee, according to the time of life, and Sarah shall have a son." She trusts in the faithfulness of God to make good of His promise. However, in Genesis 18:12 Sarah has laughed inaudibly, only to be heard by the LORD. The LORD confronts her for discounting His specific promise to her lord Abraham of her role to bear him the son. Especially, given that the previous inaudible laughter of Abraham that has been followed with the LORD insisting on "he laughs" as the word "Isaac" to become her son's name.

The LORD faults not her lord Abraham, for his inaudible laughter, whom he assures that Ishmael will not expire, rather to be replaced by Isaac in some aspect. His covenant will be established with Isaac, Sarah's son (Genesis 17:15-22, KJV). Assured enough, Sarah discounts no further but awaits the appointed time, in accordance to the time of life. On the Likert Scale, given Hebrews 11, the following scores are assigned contextual to Genesis 18: pre-conduct 1, fearful 4, promise 5, faith 5, acclaimed post-conduct 5 (See Appendix D data row **sage18**)

Annotation:

The Research Subject ID [2_Sarah] issues, crisis and narrative events variables:

Sarah, 89 years old considers herself so chronic with barrenness and with no possibility to have a son. In Genesis 18, she explicitly disclaims a nominal pre-conduct with her laughter. Without the LORD'S confrontation, her fear is implicit. The claim of the promise, faith and acclaimed post-conduct are all explicit according to the scriptures, given Hebrews 11 account.

JACOB

Jacob's faith is instructive, Hebrews 11:20-21, in differentiating the effect of inverse promises from God.

He is 130 years old abiding in the Land of Promise. Famine sets in to uproot his family of 70. Then God assures him of His presence in relocating him to and returning him from Egypt where his family will mature as a nation (Genesis 46:1-4, KJV). The trip to Egypt is with a royal escort for Jacob. On seeing each other with tears, Jacob tells Joseph how it is enough if his dad had to die, momentarily. Not yet, for the time to die in Egypt comes due 17 years later! Joseph agrees with him to carry his corpse to the Promised Land. Jacob by faith worships God for being his guide unto death, having made his son so willing to comply with his request (Genesis 47:29-31 KJV). In the closure of his life, while blessing through faith, he adopts and swaps Ephraim and Manasseh to inherit the Abrahamic covenant along with his sons (Genesis 48-49, KJV). The Faithfull God Almighty enables another royal escort to attend to his return by burial into the Land of Promise (Genesis 50, KJV). Although Jacob has secured Joseph's vow to have him buried along with Isaac and Abraham, as he concludes the blessing of all his sons, he charges all of them to comply with the burying of him in the cave that is in the field of Machpelah. On the Likert Scale, given Hebrews 11, the following scores are assigned in the context of Genesis 46: pre-conduct 5, fearful 5, promise 5, faith 5, post-conduct 5; and Genesis 48-49: pre-conduct 2, fearful 4, promise 5, faith 5, post-conduct 5; (See Appendix D data rows **jage46** and **jage48-49**).

Annotation:

The Research Subject ID [3_Jacob] issues, crisis and narrative events variables:

1, Jacob is 137 years old, and considers the prospect of being buried in Egypt. In Genesis 47, he charges Joseph with an oath to bury him in Canaan. Thereafter, he is assured and worshiped the LORD who has promised to be with his return to the promised land in Genesis 46:1-5. The scale-claims, namely: pre-conduct, crisis, promise, faith and acclaimed post-conduct are all explicit according to the scriptures, including the Hebrews 11 account.

2, Jacob blesses, with some degree of prophecy and redress, his sons, including the first two of Joseph's born in Egypt. The subject pre-conduct is of implicit disclaim with crisis is a claim. The scale item-claims of the promise, faith and acclaimed post-conduct are all explicit according to the scriptures along with the Hebrews 11 account.

JOSEPH

Joseph's faith is instructive, Hebrews 11:22, in differentiating the effect of lingering promises from God. He is 110 years old. He remembers his vow to his father enforcing Jacob's burial in the promised land, 55 years ago. As if to avoid a premature Exodus, he commands, with oath taking, his bones to remain in Egypt until when God's visiting relocates them to the land of promise, when his bones must be carried along. Joseph anticipates the delay of the children of Israel in inheriting the promised land without wavering in faith (Genesis 50:24-25, KJV). The Abrahamic 400 years clocking for freedom means that those currently under oath to carry Joseph's bones will be long dead. In Exodus 13:19, Moses takes along Joseph's bone. But Joshua delivers the bones to the promised land (Joshua 24:32, KJV). Countless Israelis must have missed similar hopeful treatment of Joseph's bones as they have expired in Egypt and in the wilderness. On the Likert Scale, given Hebrews 11, the following scores are assigned in the context of Genesis 50: pre-conduct 2, fearful 3, promise 5, faith 5, post-conduct 5. (See Appendix D data row **joge50**).

Annotation:

The Research Subject ID [4_Joseph] issues, crisis and narrative events variables:

Joseph, at 110 years of age, imitates his father Jacob. It has been 55 years since Jacob adjured the family to make the land of promise the final resting place of his bones. However, Joseph's dead body will linger in an Egyptian grave, but in anticipation of the Exodus many years to come. The subject pre-conduct is of an implicit disclaim with an indeterminate fearfulness. The scale item-claims of the promise, faith and acclaimed post-conduct are all explicit according to the scriptures along with the Hebrews 11 account.

MOSES

The Hebrews epistle lists 3 instances of faith on Moses and 2 more on Moses inclusive of the Israelites. The chiastic listings of this section demonstrate application of faith that resolves WHEN imperial wrath assails discriminately those identified with the reproach of the invisible Christ (Hebrews 11:26-27 vis-a-vis Hebrews 13:13 KJV). Moses's name meaning "drawn out of water" brings to memory the faith of the parents in God over such a promising looking child challenge with Pharaoh's wrath by infanticide. Similarly, the Herodian wrath by infanticide prompts baby Jesus' escape to Egypt. In Duet 18:15, Moses assures the Israelites the coming of Christ as prophet like him. Coincidentally, in a general recall is the admonishment of Christ that "if they have persecuted me, they will also persecute you" (John 15:20 KJV). At maturity, Moses choses to relinquish the Egyptian's esteemed identity for "the reproach of Christ" (Hebrews 11:26, KJV). Didactic to faith definition, (viz. Hebrews 11:1, KJV), Moses has the enduring faith ascertained in the binary as SUBSTANCE of things hope for, i. e. "greater riches than treasures in Egypt" (Hebrews 11:26, KJV) and the EVIDENCE "as seeing him who is invisible" (Hebrews 11:27, KJV). In the application level of faith, the "wrath of the king" (Hebrews 11:27, KJV) is nothing to be feared. The prophetic inspiration and privilege of Moses are unique and vast as the writer of the beginning of creation, the in-betweens, to the Messianic advent. On the Likert Scale, given Hebrews 11 & Acts 7, the following scores are assigned in the context of Exodus 2:2: pre-conduct 3, fearful 2, promise 4, faith 5, post-conduct 5; Exodus 2:11: pre-conduct 3, fearful 2, promise 4, faith 5, post-conduct 5; Exodus 2:14-15: pre-conduct 1, fearful 1, promise 4, faith 4, post-conduct 4; Exodus 12: pre-conduct 2, fearful 4, promise 5, faith 5, post-conduct 5; and Exodus 14: pre-conduct 4, fearful 5, promise 5, faith 5, post-conduct 5; (See Appendix D data rows **moex2@2**, **moex2@11**, **moex2@14**, **moex12** and **moex14**).

Annotation:

The Research Subject ID [5_Moses] issues, crisis and narrative events variables:

1, Moses is lovely looking to God. He bears the look of a promising child to the faith parents and the foster parent. The birth and drawn out of water parents, the midwives and the maidens encircle dramatically the boy to escape the wrath of a king. The subject's pre-conduct is scored indeterminate and crisis is scored with an implicit disclaim. The score for promise is of an implicit claim. The scores for faith, and acclaimed post-conduct are all with explicit claims according to the scriptures given the Hebrews 11 account.

2, Moses has grown to be forty with a flashback on the cruelty of hate and slavery. He takes charge to defend an abused Israeli, having denounced the cruel Pharaoh's household by faith. The subject's pre-conduct is scored indeterminate and crisis is scored with an implicit disclaim. The score for promise is of an implicit claim. The scores for faith, and acclaimed post-conduct are all with explicit claims according to the scriptures given the Hebrews 11 account.

3, Moses thinks, he has started a revolution by killing the Egyptian inadvertently, but to his surprise, another Israelite wants to turn him over to Pharaoh. His real own has rejected his intervention, he has fled to the unknown by faith. The subject nominal pre-conduct and crisis are scored with explicit disclaims. The scores for promise, faith, and acclaimed post-conduct are all with implicit claims according to the scriptures given in the book of Acts 7 and Hebrews 11 account.

4, More than the wrath of a king, Moses deals with the wrath of God, death of the firstborn. The wrath spears only those with blood marks on their door posts and in compliance to the departure preparations. By faith Moses kept the Passover. The subject's nominal pre-conduct is scored with implicit disclaim and the crisis with implicit claim. The scores for the promise, faith, and acclaimed post-conduct are all with explicit claims according to the scriptures given the Hebrews 11 account.

5, The Israelites have the army of Pharaoh in the rear and the Red Sea in the front. In exchange of the cry and trepidation, God orders the Israelites to step into the sea by faith which quickens the sea into parting wide asunder and surrendering the seabed hardened dry for the easy pedestrian and wagon trafficking. The subject's nominal pre-conduct is scored with an implicit claim. The scores for the crisis, promise, faith, and acclaimed post-conduct are all with explicit claims according to the scriptures given the Hebrews 11 account.

REHAB

The chiastic structure of Hebrews 11 puts the fall of the walls of Jericho and Rehab's accounts with faith application WHEN confronted with a sovereign wrath. The wrath of Pharaoh has been overtaken by the wrath of God at Passover and in the Red Sea. The iniquity of Jericho is full as measured for the Amorites (Genesis 15:16; Joshua 2:10 KJV). "(T)he utmost wrath has come upon them" (1 Thessalonians 2:16 KJV). Like the Passover blood mark on the door posts, the line of scarlet thread becomes the mark for the spies, and Rehab with her household to escape an impending wrath, human or divine respectively.

> Behold, when we come into the land, thou shalt bind this line of scarlet thread in the window which thou didst let us down by and thou shalt bring thy father, and thy mother, and thy brethren, and all thy father's household, home unto thee, (Joshua 2:18, KJV).

Given Hebrews 11:3 KJV, at the definition level, by faith Rehab understands, the evidence of the invisible God, to express in Joshua 2:9–12 KJV: "I know the LORD has given you the land," "(w)e have heard how the LORD dried up the water of the Red Sea." And in the account, she understands the Israelites' LORD as "God in Heaven above and in earth beneath." Following her understanding of faith is her application of faith to the oath by the LORD using the line of scarlet thread. On the Likert Scale, given Hebrews 11 account, the following scores are assigned in the context of Joshua 2:8-21: pre-conduct 5, fearful 5, promise 5, faith 5, post-conduct 5; (See Appendix D data row **rejo2**).

Annotation:

The Research Subject ID [6_Rehab] issues, crisis, and narrative events variables:
The reputation of God in Exodus has reached Jericho before the spies show up. The iniquity of Jericho is full for the impending wrath but Rehab, the harlot has heard enough to believe in God for her household's redemption. The subject item scores for the pre-conduct, crisis, promise, faith, and acclaimed post-conduct are all with explicit claims according to the scriptures given the Hebrews 11 account.

BARAK

The didactic-chiastic structure of Hebrews 11 puts Barak's agency of faith in a distinguishable (WHICH) category, a victim or victor for God, like Abel or Enoch. Gideon and Barak are victors, listed as a pair in reverse order, who through faith "subdued kingdoms," given the adjacent first listing of the accomplishments, (Hebrews 11:32-33, KJV). For twenty years Jabin has oppressed Israel. In answer to their prayers, the Lord delivers them through the faith of Barak nurtured by Deborah the prophetess. In Judges 4:14 KJV: "then Deborah said to Barak, 'Go! This is the day the LORD has given Sisera into your hands. Has not the LORD gone ahead of you?' So, Barak went down Mount Tabor, with ten thousand men following him." However, deliverance from oppression is not always the case in which the agency of faith must sustain the victims "who are not accepting deliverance; that they might obtain a better resurrection:" (Hebrews 11: 35 KJV) On the Likert Scale, given Hebrews 11, the following scores are assigned in the context of Judges 4; pre-conduct 3, fearful 4, promise 5, faith 5, post-conduct 5. (See Appendix D data row **baju4**).

Annotation:

The Research Subject ID [7_Barak] issues, crisis and narrative events variables

Barak though reluctant at first finally believes in Deborah prophetic promise of God to use him to subdue Jabin and liberate Israel (Judges 4:14). The subject scores for the pre-conduct is indeterminate, crisis score implicit claim;

while promise, faith, and acclaimed post-conduct are all with explicit claims scores according to the scriptures given the Hebrews 11 account.

GIDEON

The didactic-chiastic structure of Hebrews 11 puts Gideon's agency of faith in a distinguishable (WHICH) category, a victim or victor for God, like Abel or Enoch. Gideon and Barak are victors, listed as a pair in reverse order, who through faith "subdued kingdoms," given the adjacent first listing of the accomplishments, (Hebrews 11:32-33 KJV). For seven oppressive years the Midianites have caused Israelites to shelter in caves at a distance, Judges 6. In Judges 7:7 KJV is the promise: "And the LORD said unto Gideon, By the three hundred men that lapped will I save you and deliver the Midianites into thine hand: and let all the other people go every man unto his place." Unlike the help Deborah renders to strengthen Barak's agency of faith with 10,000 men, Gideon receives direct help to assure himself of God through faith to subdue the Midianites even with 300 men. On the Likert Scale, given Hebrews 11, the following scores are assigned in the context of Judges 6-8: pre-conduct 3, fearful 4, promise

5, faith 5, post-conduct 5. (See Appendix D data row **giju7**)

Annotation:

The Research Subject ID [8_Gideon] issues, crisis and narrative events variables

With all the flea bargaining for assurance, Gideon brings along eventually, the agency of his faith in God to subdue the enemies with just 300 men in conflict with thousands of the Midianites. The subject scores for the pre-conduct score is indeterminate, crisis score implicit claim; while promise, faith, and acclaimed post-conduct are all with explicit claims scores according to the scriptures given the Hebrews 11 account.

JEPHTHAH

The didactic/chiastic structure of Hebrews 11 puts Jephthah's agency of faith in a distinguishable (WHICH) category, a victim or victor for God, like Abel or Enoch. Samson and Jephthah are victors, listed as a pair in reverse order, who through faith "wrought righteousness," given the adjacent second listing of the accomplishments, (Hebrews 11:32-33, KJV). In Judges 11:27, "the LORD the Judge be judge this day between the children of Israel and the children of Ammon." In the controversy with the Amorites, faith and defense in the Abrahamic promise and inheritance are overwhelming but disregarded by his opponent (Judges 11:14-28, KJV). Also, he thinks that a vow of triumph will seal the doom of the Amorites. He becomes victorious subjugating twenty cities of the Amorites. His daughter preemptively celebrates his father's victory that brings the unintended "trial of cruel mocking" (Hebrews 11:36, KJV) to his family. He does not rescind his vow. Yearly, for four days, the daughters of Israel lament the fate of his virgin daughter as a victim of his success. On the Likert Scale, given Hebrews 11, the following scores are assigned in the context of Judges 11: pre-conduct 4, fearful 2, promise 5, faith 5, post-conduct 5. (See Appendix D data row **jeju11**)

Annotation:

The Research Subject ID [9_Jephthah] issues, crisis and narrative events variables

Jephthah negotiates from the position of absolute trust in God unafraid of the Amorites. However, to hedge his triumph he makes a vow with an intended outcome for the daughter. He keeps his vow anyway. The subject score for the pre-conduct is an implicit claim, crisis score is an implicit disclaim; while promise, faith, and acclaimed post-conduct are all with explicit claims scores according to the scriptures given the Hebrews 11 account.

SAMSON

The didactic/chiastic structure of Hebrews 11 puts Samson's agency of faith in a distinguishable (WHICH) category, a victim or victor for God, like Abel or Enoch. Samson and Jephthah are victors, listed as a pair in reverse order, who through faith "wrought righteousness," given the adjacent second listing of the accomplishments, (Hebrews 11:32-33, KJV). Samson's birth is announced by an angel. He is committed as a Nazarite growing up. He rules Israel for twenty years. His jilted marriage with a Philistine woman becomes the precursor of fatal conflicts with the Philistines who are in controversy of national injustice to Israel and personal injustice to Samson. For Samson, God is the Shepherd that leads beside the still waters when athirst. He prays,

> Thou hast given this great deliverance into the hand of thy servant: and now shall I die for thirst, and fall into the hand of the uncircumcised? But God clave a hollow place that was in the jaw, and there came water thereout; and when he had drunk, his spirit came again, and he revived: wherefore he called the name thereof Enhakkore, which is in Lehi unto this day (Judges 15:18-19, KJV).

Blind and in apparent defeat, he prays again, "O Lord GOD, remember me, I pray thee, and strengthen me, I pray thee, only this once, O God, that I may be at once avenged of the Philistines for my two eyes" (Judges 16:28, KJV). The "trial of cruel mocking and scourging" (Hebrews 11:36, KJV) are detrimental to Samson but it enforces his personal and national justice against the annihilated Philistines (Judges 16:30, KJV). On the Likert Scale, given Hebrews 11, the following scores are assigned in the context of Judges 16: pre-conduct 5, fearful 1, promise 5, faith 5, post-conduct 5. (See Appendix D data row **saju16**).

Annotation:

The Research Subject ID [10_Samson] issues, crisis and narrative events variables

The call of Samson is right from birth, unafraid. He trusts God for water to drink and vengeance for his and national enemies, the Philistines. Even dying, he kills more than when living by faith to redress injustice. The subject's score for the pre-conduct is an explicit claim, crisis score is an explicit disclaim; while promise, faith, and acclaimed post-conduct are all with explicit claim scores according to the scriptures given the Hebrews 11 account.

SAMUEL

The didactic-chiastic structure of Hebrews 11 puts Samuel's agency of faith in a distinguishable (WHICH) category, a victim or victor for God, like Abel or Enoch. David and Samuel are victors, listed as a pair in reverse order, who through faith "obtained promises," given the adjacent third listing of the accomplishments, (Hebrews 11:32-33, KJV). Beyond the pairing, Samuel also belongs to the prophets as a group with no personal identities to march the listing of accomplishments that follow in 1 Samuel 12:11, Samuel is listed as a deliverer like Gideon, Barak, and Jephthah. Rightly, 1 Samuel 1:20 in Psalm 99:6 he is listed with Moses and Aaron as prayerful with answers. And he is overwhelmed in prayer with the Israelites' request for a monarchy, moreover the Lord puts the responsibilities on him to give them a king (1 Samuel 8:22 KJV). While trusting the Lord for help, Samuel obtains the promise in regarding to the monarchy: "Tomorrow about this time I will send thee a man out of the land of Benjamin, and thou shalt anoint him" (1 Samuel 9:16, KJV). Eventually, king Saul is rejected, David is anointed which allows Samuel to accomplish the Israeli transition to the monarchy as promised. Ironically, Samuel is almost implicated by his sons, Joel and Abiah, with a near misconduct to the Eli's children's. Apparently, both God and Samuel have been rejected, respectively. Considering the closure of the crisis in 1 Samuel 12:18 KJV, "So Samuel called unto the LORD; and the LORD sent thunder and rain that day: and all the people greatly feared the LORD and Samuel." On the Likert Scale, given Hebrews 11, the following scores are assigned in the context of 1 Samuel 8-12: pre-conduct 4, fearful 4, promise 5, faith 5, post-conduct 5. (See Appendix D data row **sa1sa9**).

Annotation:

The Research Subject ID [11_Samuel] issues, crisis and narrative events variables

Samuel's agency of faith transitions Israel from theocracy as he obtains the promise to institute the monarchy. He receives and anoints Saul abortively. He inquires and anoints David that holds after God's heart. The subject's score for the pre-conduct and crisis score are with implicit claims; while promise, faith, and acclaimed post-conduct are all with explicit claim scores according to the scriptures given the Hebrews 11 account.

DAVID

The didactic/chiastic structure of Hebrews 11 puts David's agency of faith in a distinguishable (WHICH) category, a victim or victor for God, like Abel or Enoch. David and Samuel are victors, listed as a pair in reverse order, who through faith "obtained promises," given the adjacent third listing of the accomplishments, (Hebrews 11:32-33, KJV). Anointed but without coronation, David conquers Goliath by faith to show that God is the Deliverer of his and the Israelites. Currently the LORD has subdued King David's enemies. Then King David obliges himself to build for God a better dwelling than his own. The LORD retorts masterfully, instead, King David obtains a promise, the assurance of his Dynasty. David seizes on the promise by a prayer of faith:

> For thou, O LORD of hosts, God of Israel, hast revealed to thy servant, saying, I will build thee a house: therefore, hath thy servant found in his heart to pray this prayer unto thee. And now, O Lord GOD, thou art that God, and thy words be true, and thou hast promised this goodness unto thy servant: therefore, now let it please thee to bless the house of thy servant, that it may continue forever before thee: for thou, O Lord GOD, hast spoken it: and with thy blessing let the house of thy servant be blessed forever (2 Samuel 7:27-29, KJV).

The Davidic covenant presents a flashback of King Saul's misses that put Jonathan under the demise of Saul. Though a victim, Jonathan's faith too will be remembered like those in "bonds and imprisonment" (Hebrews 11:36, KJV). Earlier in their existence,

> Jonathan and David made a covenant because he loved him as his own soul. And Jonathan stripped himself of the robe that was upon him, and gave it to David, and his garments, even to his sword, and to his bow, and to his girdle (1 Samuel 18:3-4, KJV).

On the Likert Scale, given Hebrews 11, the scores are assigned in the context of 2 Samuel 7: pre-conduct 2, fearful 4, promise 5, faith 5, post-conduct 5. (See Appendix D data row **da2sa7**).

Annotation:

The Research Subject ID [12_David] issues, crisis and narrative events variables

David wants the pre-eminence of God's dwelling. Instead, he obtains a promise for his perpetual dynasty. The Davidic Covenant is premium which he further embraces in prayer. The subject's score for the pre-conduct is an implicit disclaim, crisis score is an implicit claim; while promise, faith, and acclaimed post-conduct are all with explicit claim scores according to the scriptures given the Hebrews 11 account.

RESEARCH VARIABLE ANALYSIS AND RESULT

ANALYSIS

The SPSS 5 items Likert scale output for *Cronbach's Alpha* is **.523** and *Cronbach's Alpha Based on Standardized Items* is **.764**. The latter level of Reliability (Alpha output) applies the correlations among items the former covariances among items. http://www-01.ibm.com/support/docview.wss?uid=swg21479940.

The Alpha coefficient score **.764** is acceptable given the standardizing assumption of equal variance among the items. The output shows Pearson Correlation is **.687** significant at the 0.01 level (2-tailed) among items of faith and post-conduct. There is another Pearson Correlation output of **.615** significant at the 0.01 level (2-tailed) among items of crisis and promise. The SPSS output tables of the Descriptive Statistics and Correlations are hereby provided:

Table 3.20 The Descriptive Statistics: Bible Subjects Data

	Mean	Std. Deviation	N
Subject allows a nominal pre-conduct	3.11	1.243	19
Subject senses a crisis	3.47	1.307	19
Subject embraces a promise	4.84	.375	19
Subject copes by faith	4.89	.315	19
Subject presents an acclaimed post-conduct	4.95	.229	19

Table 3.21a The Correlations Bible Subjects Data

		Subject allows a nominal pre-conduct	Subject senses a crisis	Subject embraces a promise
Subject allows a nominal pre-conduct	Pearson Correlation	1	.173	.276
	Sig. (2-tailed)		.479	.252
	N	19	19	19
Subject senses a crisis	Pearson Correlation	.173	1	.615[**]
	Sig. (2-tailed)	.479		.005
	N	19	19	19
Subject embraces a promise	Pearson Correlation	.276	.615[**]	1
	Sig. (2-tailed)	.252	.005	
	N	19	19	19
Subject copes by faith	Pearson Correlation	.313	.128	.322
	Sig. (2-tailed)	.191	.602	.179

	N	19	19	19
Subject presents an acclaimed post-conduct	Pearson Correlation	.410	.458[*]	.544[*]
	Sig. (2-tailed)	.081	.048	.016
	N	19	19	19

Table 3.21b The Correlations Bible Subjects Data

		Subject copes by faith	Subject presents an acclaimed post–conduct
Subject allows a nominal pre–conduct	Pearson Correlation	.313	.410
	Sig. (2–tailed)	.191	.081
	N	19	19
Subject senses a crisis	Pearson Correlation	.128	.458[*]
	Sig. (2–tailed)	.602	.048
	N	19	19
Subject embraces a promise	Pearson Correlation	.322	.544[*]
	Sig. (2–tailed)	.179	.016
	N	19	19

Subject copes by faith	Pearson Correlation	1	.687[**]
	Sig. (2-tailed)		.001
	N	19	19
Subject presents an acclaimed post-conduct	Pearson Correlation	.687[**]	1
	Sig. (2-tailed)	.001	
	N	19	19

**. Correlation is significant at the 0.01 level (2-tailed).

*. Correlation is significant at the 0.05 level (2-tailed).

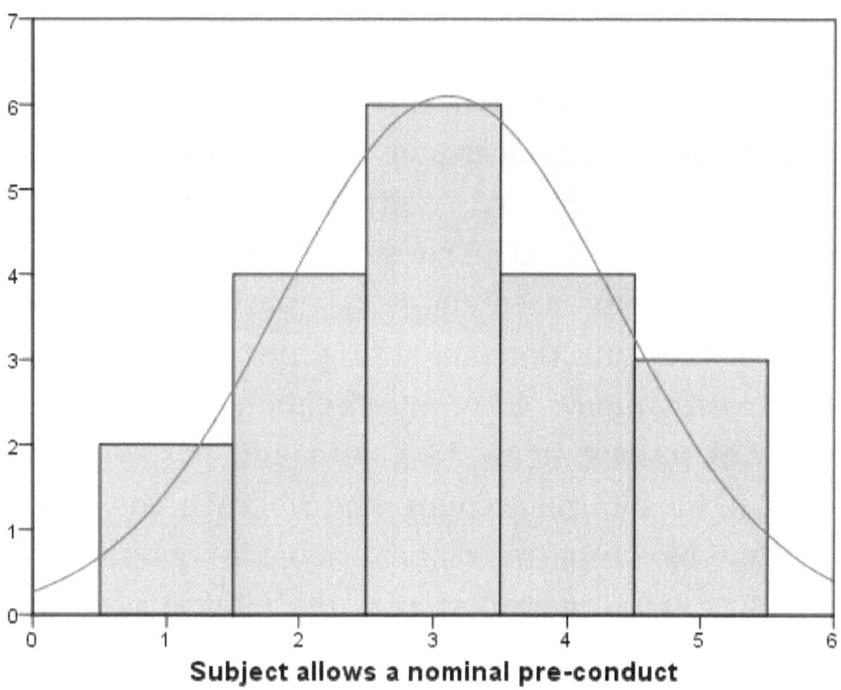

FIGURE 3:2 TWELVE BIBLICAL SUBJECTS 19 INCIDENCES 5 ITEMS DATA

X-AXIS
1=NOMINAL-CONDUCT
2=IN-CRISIS
3=AS-PROMISEE
4=BY-FAITH
5=ACCLAIMED-CONDUCT

CONCLUSION

Nineteen purposeful samples of incidental events are observed in the written biblical record of twelve Hebrews Chapter 11 subjects concerning their pre-conduct, life crisis, promises claimed, faith professed and the acclaimed post-conduct. The statistical output of the Likert scale 5 items used suggests a positive answer to one of the study questions regarding the biblical subjects under investigation.[10] The investigation is about the correlations among items like faith and post-conduct affirmed in the biblical account. The biblical account also states that by faith the biblical subjects obtain good reports. The investigation studies the biblical narrative contexts that indicate the prevailing conduct, crisis and promises leading to affirmed lifestyle. In view of scholastic cautions, the investigator has not advanced the merit of Cronbach's Alpha coefficient and Pearson correlation for a theological argument but a philosophical inherence. The reliability of all biblical subjects' narratives is absolute whereas the method and result of investigation are prone to a disagreeable instrument or measure of reliability.

---

[10] The twelve OT exemplars with sampled combined nineteen incidences by faith

CHAPTER 4: LIABLE PROMISES PREVENIENT TO THE SPIRITUAL FORMATION DISCIPLINES FOR THE EVANGELICAL FAITH WALKTHROUGH

The evangelic person acts by faith to please God in every phase of development spiritually. Therefore, faith that comes by hearing the word or promise of God are necessary to precede the evangelic endeavors, including Spiritual Formation Disciplines in a cognitive framework as a stepwise faith learning through the assurance of things hoped for and the evidence of the invisible hand of God. This walkthrough chapter is an attempt to suggest or inform stepwise faith in some bible Liable Promises relevant to the classic Spiritual Formation Discipline for the evangelicals.

?1: *WHAT* IS A LIABLE PROMISE AS IT *RELATES* TO SPIRITUAL FORMATION DISCIPLINES, PRAYER AND FASTING

THE SUPPLIES AND REWARD

God offers the invitation to pray with a promise. But the offeree must come to grip with the offer as real as stated. "And all things, whatsoever ye shall ask in prayer, believing, ye shall receive," (Matthew 21:22 KJV). In case the offeree is further committed to fasting along while making a claim, there is a reward. "But thou, when thou fastest, anoint thine head, and wash thy face; That thou appear not unto men to fast, but unto thy Father which is in secret: and thy Father, which seeth in secret, shall reward thee openly," (Matthew 6:17-18, KJV).

Reasonably, Prayer and Fasting assist the spiritual development inwardly to care for the desires of life with the divine promissory of supplies and reward. Consider the following evidential scriptures: "He that spared not his own Son, but delivered him up for us all, how shall he not with him also freely give us all things?" (Romans 8:32 KJV). "Delight thyself also in the LORD; and he shall give thee the desires of thine heart," (Psalm 37:4, KJV). "You have granted him his heart's desire and have not withheld the request of his lips." (Psalms 21:2, KJV). There are some complications to deal with to avoid exasperation with prayers and fasting hindered:

> You covet but you cannot get what you want, so you quarrel and fight. You do not have because you do not ask God. When you ask, you do not receive, because you ask with wrong motives, that you may spend what you get on your pleasures, (James 4:2-3, NIV).

> Behold, the LORD'S hand is not shortened, that it cannot save; neither his ear heavy, that it cannot hear: But your iniquities have separated between you and your God, and your sins have hid his face from you, that he will not hear, (Isaiah 59:1-2, KJV).

The Scripture assures God that has the integrity to fulfill his promise to those with the integrity of heart for what they ask to receive, what they seek to find, and what door they knock to open. "He (Abraham) staggered not at the promise of God through unbelief; but was strong in faith, giving glory to God," (Romans 4:20, KJV), while making God his "exceeding great reward," (Genesis 15:1, KJV).

?2: *WHICH* LIABLE PROMISE FACTOR IS *REVIEWED* FOR SPIRITUAL FORMATION DISCIPLINES, MEDITATION AND STUDY

THE APPROVAL AND PROSPERITY

The Holy Spirit convicts a person with the scriptural promise that fits a person's spiritual need. The Psalmist examines the bible, "My eyes stay open through the watches of the night, that I may meditate on your promises," (Psalms 119:148 NIV). Furthermore, it is required for approval to study, "rightly dividing the word of truth", (2 Timothy 2:15, KJV). Meditating and Studying assist the spiritual development internally to inform the appropriate desire with divine promissory for returns and commendation. Given the instruction that,

> this book of the law shall not depart out of thy mouth; but thou shalt meditate therein day and night, that thou mayest observe to do according to all that is written therein: for then thou shalt make thy way prosperous, and then thou shalt have good success, (Joshua 1:8, KJV).

It is complicating or blindsiding to consider divine promissory without Christ as the bases of divine integrity (Romans 8;32, KJV). God's promises are yea in Christ. Jesus cautions, "You study the Scriptures diligently because you think that in them you have eternal life. These are the very Scriptures that testify about me, yet you refuse to come to me to have life," (John5:39-40, KJV). The meditation and study help in the renewing and reviewing divine promissory which is effectual at a given situation in a personal or community life.

?3: *WHEN* IS A LIABLE PROMISE FAITH *RESOLVED* BY SPIRITUAL FORMATION DISCIPLINES, SUBMISSION AND SERVICE

THE HUMBLITY AND HONOR

Christ serves meekly and lowly at heart. "Humble yourselves before the Lord, and he will lift you up," (James 4:10 KJV). "Whoever serves me must follow me; and where I am, my servant also will be. My Father will honor the one who serves me," (John 12:26 KJV). Submission and Service assist the spiritual development externally to cope with the pride of life subsumed in the divine promissory of exaltation and honor. The mind set as a servant of God, yielding to God, and as a human breed, humbling oneself must prevail in accordance with Christ's framework in (Philippians 2:5–8, KJV). Pride of life is very elusive to make claim of, and Satan knows it. "For who maketh thee to differ from another? and what hast thou that thou didst not receive? now if thou didst receive it, why dost thou glory, as if thou hadst not received it?" (1 Corinthians 4:7, KJV). To be submissive while serving by faith obscures greatness when undertaking a humble walk with God.

?4: *WHY* IS A LIABLE PROMISE FIDELITY *DIFFERENTIATED* IN SPIRITUAL FORMATION DISCIPLINES, SIMPLICITY AND SOLITUDE

THE PLAINNESS AND FORTITUDE

Sometimes, "the worries of this life and the deceitfulness of wealth choke the word, making it unfruitful," (Matthew 13:22, NIV).

> Keep your lives free from the love of money and be content with what you have, because God has said, 'Never will I leave you; never will I forsake you.' So, we say with confidence, 'The Lord is my helper; I will not be afraid. What can mere mortals do to me?' (Hebrews 13:5–6, NIV).

Simplicity and Solitude assist in the spiritual development externally to ensure one's poise with the divine promissory of help and fortitude. "Why, my soul, are you downcast? Why so disturbed within me? Put your hope in God, for I will yet praise him, my Savior and my God," (Psalms 42:5 NIV). Sometimes it is a matter of encouraging oneself in the Lord even by self-talk not to fear any evil since God is faithful, even when one is unfaithful. Job admonishes himself, "though He slays me yet will I trust Him." The Lord Jesus that asks why hast thou forsaken me, rejoins with the statement – "into thy hand I commit my Spirit." In all temptations common to man, faithful God provides a way out of a mortal jeopardy.

?5: *WHERE* IS A LIABLE PROMISE *ACCOUNTING* FOR TRUST THROUGH SPIRITUAL FORMATION DISCIPLINES, CONFESSION AND GUIDANCE

THE PROOFING AND ADVANCING

Sin, original or corporate, dulls sensitivity to personal sins.

If we claim to be without sin, we deceive ourselves and the truth is not in us. If we confess our sins, he is faithful and just and will forgive us our sins and purify us from all unrighteousness. If we claim we have not sinned, we make him out to be a liar and his word is not in us, (1 John 1:8-10, NIV).

"Trust in the LORD with all thine heart; and lean not unto thine own understanding. In all thy ways acknowledge him, and he shall direct thy paths," (Proverbs 3:5-6, KJV). Confession and Guidance assist the spiritual development corporately to hold the community account with the divine promissory of cleansing and directing. Prophet Isaiah confesses, "Woe to me!" I cried. "I am ruined! For I am a man of unclean lips, and I live among a people of unclean lips, and my eyes have seen the King, the LORD Almighty," (Isaiah 6:5, NIV). Where idolatry is rampant due to covetousness, due to the lust of the eye,

Isaiah's eyes envision the Lord of glory that implicates the lips of his and the community in sinful communication or social media. With confession Isaiah is cleansed with evangelic response to be sent on a revival mission to the indifferent society where skeptics defy the righteousness as the principle that exalts a nation, (Proverbs 14:34, KJV).

?6: *WHOSE* LIABLE PROMISE PARTNER IS *VENERATED* BY SPIRITUAL FORMATION DISCIPLINES, CELEBRATION AND WORSHIP

THE MAGNIFICATION AND GLORIFICATION

"Let them shout for joy, and be glad, that favor my righteous cause: yea, let them say continually, Let the LORD be magnified, which hath pleasure in the prosperity of his servant," (Psalms 35:27, KJV).

Let us hold fast the profession of our faith without wavering; (for he is faithful that promised;) And let us consider one another to provoke unto love and to good works: Not forsaking the assembling of ourselves together, as the manner of some is; but exhorting one another: and so much the more, as ye see the day approaching, (Hebrews 10: 23-25, KJV).

Celebration and Worship assist the spiritual development individually and corporately to glorify the Almighty God for the divine promissory in prospering and evaluating the seekers He sought for His Worship.

And because of his glory and excellence, he has given us great and precious promises. These are the promises that enable you to share his divine nature and escape the world's corruption caused by human desires, (2 Peter 1:4, NLT).

In a local congregation, the figurative wheats and tears are in worship attendance. Nevertheless, the true worshipers will worship God in Spirit and truth, for they are the kind of worshipers the Father seeks (John 4;23-24, NIV). Ultimately Spiritual Formation Disciplines must cultivate spiritually the true worshippers as the treasures of God.

APPENDIX A

Data Template for the Rating of Variables of Narrative Events					
Item: **"To-what extent"**[11]	Explicit Disclaim	Implicit Disclaim	Indeterminate	Implicit Claim	Explicit Claim
Subject's pre-conduct is nominal	1	2	3	4	5
Subject is in a crisis or fearful	1	2	3	4	5
Subject is aware of a promise	1	2	3	4	5
Subject is exercising faith	1	2	3	4	5
Subject's post-conduct is acclaimed	1	2	3	4	5
Narrative Content Analysis Annotation: The Research Subject ID [...]					

---

[11] Dawn L Eubanks, et al. "Time to Create" *In Creative and Leadership in Science, Technology, and Innovation*. Ed. Steven Hemlin 185-272 (New York: Routledge. 2013), 198.

APPENDIX B

Koleosho, Olusanya. "Transforming the Educational Experience with Cognitive Content Crafting Construct". *Poster*. Vancouver: Third Annual WebCT Conference, 2001, June 22–27

A Poster Extract: Pilot Study

Best Fit Entry Level to a Body of Information			Best Fit to the Bloom's Cognitive Level	
Bloom's Level	Word Verb Association		Interrogative Pronoun	% Rated of the Level
Knowledge	Define		What	87.5
Comprehension	Identify		Which	75
Application	Choose		When	87.5
Analysis	Examine		Why	87.5
Synthesis	Collect		Where	62.5
Evaluation	Appraise		Whose	62.5

APPENDIX C

**Classical Spiritual Formation Disciplines and Suggested Divine Promissory
[For those Seeking God not in Vain]**

Discipline[12]	Area[13]	Promissory	Scripture (KJV)	Overcoming
Meditation	Inward	For Profiting	Psalm 119:148, 19:13, Timothy 4:15, Joshua 1:8	Flesh (not by bread alone)
Prayer	Inward	For Supplies	Romans 8:33, Matthew 7:7-8	Flesh (not by bread alone
Fasting	Inward	For Reward	Matthew 6:17-18	Flesh (not by bread alone
Study	Inward	For Commendation	2 Timothy 2:15	Flesh (not by bread alone
Simplicity	Outward	For Help	Hebrews 13:5-6	Pride (tempt not God)
Solitude	Outward	For Strength	Genesis 32:26-28; Daniel 10:8	Pride (tempt not God)
Submission	Outward	For Uplift	Philippians 2:5-9; 2Corinthians 12:7	Pride (tempt not God)

---

[12] Richard J. Foster. *The Celebration of Discipline: The Path to Spiritual growth* (San Francisco: Harper Collins 1998), Content page.

[13] Ibid., Content page.

Service	Outward	For Honor	John 12:26	Pride (tempt not God)
Confession	Corporate	For Cleansing	Romans 2:4; 6:14; 1 John 1:9-10; 1 Timothy 4:8	Eye (get thee hence Satan)
Worship	Corporate	For Valuing	John 4:23-24; Hebrews 10:23-25	Eye (get thee hence Satan)
Guidance	Corporate	For Navigating	John 16:13; Psalms 32:8	Eye (get thee hence Satan)
Celebration	Corporate	For Prospering	Psalms 35:27	Eye (get thee hence Satan)

APPENDIX D

Research Data of the Bible Heroes of faith Incidence by Scale

Subj-Inst	Pre-conduct	In-crisis	As-Promisee	By-Faith	Post-conduct
Abge12	3	3	5	5	5
Abge22	4	4	5	5	5
Abge23	3	5	5	4	5
Sage18	1	4	5	5	5
Jage46	5	5	5	5	5
Jage4849	2	4	5	5	5
Joge50	2	3	5	5	5
Moex2@2	3	2	4	5	5
Moex2@11	3	2	4	5	5
Moex2@14	1	1	4	4	4
Moex12	2	4	5	5	5
Moex14	4	5	5	5	5
Rajo2	5	5	5	5	5
Baju4H11	3	4	5	5	5
Giju4H11	3	4	5	5	5
Jeju11H11	4	2	5	5	5
Saju16	5	1	5	5	5
Sa1sa8-12	4	4	5	5	5
Da2sa7	2	4	5	5	5

BIBLIOGRAPHY

Anderson, Lori W., Krathwohl, David R. Editors. *A Taxonomy for Learning, Teaching, and Assessing: A Revision of Bloom's Taxonomy of Educational Objectives*. New York: Longman, 2001.

Benun, Ronald. "Evil and the Disruption of Order a Structural Analysis of the Acrostics in the First Book of Psalms" (2017).
http://www.jhsonline.org/cocoon/JHS/a055.html
Accessed November 20, 2017.

Cockerill, Gareth Lee. *The New International Commentary on the New Testament: The Epistle to the Hebrews* Grand Rapids: Wm. B. Eerdmans Publication, 2012.

Eubanks, Dawn L. et al. "Time to Create" *In Creative and Leadership in Science, Technology and Innovation*. Ed. Steven Hemlin 185-272 New York: Routledge. 2013.

Forster, Richard J. *Celebration of Discipline: The Path to Spiritual Growth-20th Anniversary*. San Francisco: HarperCollins, 1998.
__________________. "Spiritual Formation Agenda: Richard Foster Shares His Three
Priorities for the Next 30 Years." *Christianity Today* (January 2009): 29-32.
Forster, Richard J., Willard, Dallas, Tenant, Agnieszka "Christian Life; Spiritual Formation; Discipleship." *Christianity Today* 49 no 10 (2005): 42-44.

Health, David Mark. "Chiastic Structures in Hebrews: A Study of Form and Function in Biblical Discourse" *Dissertation presented for the Degree of Doctor of Philosophy in Biblical Languages* at the University of Stellenbosch South Africa. March (2011), Abstract.

Koleosho, Olusanya. Poster Session: "Transforming the Educational Experience with Cognitive Content Crafting Construct." *Third Annual WebCT Conference, June 22-27, 2001,* Vancouver BC.

Nuyten, Gill. "Secret of the Hebrew letter Shin" (2017) http://www.thelivingword.org.au/grand-design/session39.php accessed November 21, 2017

Rhee, Victor (Sung Yul). "Chiasm and the Concept of Faith in Hebrews 11." *Bibliotheca Sacra* 155 (July- September 1998): 327-45.

Smith, James Bryan, with Graybeal, Lynda, and Forster, Richard J. *A Spiritual Formation Workbook: Small-Group Resources for Nurturing Christian Growth. A Revised Edition.* San Francisco: Harper Collins, 1999.

Smith, W.M. "Promise." In *Evangelical Dictionary of Theology, 2nd Edition,* ed. Walter A Elwell. 959-960. Grand Rapids: Baker Academic, 2001.

Spurstowe, William. *The Wells of Salvation Opened.* Coconut Creek: Puritan Publication, 2012.

Wallace, Daniel B. Greek Grammar: *Beyond the Basics: An Exegetical Syntax of the New Testament.* Grand Rapids: Zondernvan, 1996.

Warren, Rick. *The Purpose Driven Life: What on Earth Am I Here for?* Grand Rapids: Zondervan, 2002.
_________________ "Pastor Ricks Daily Hope: Our Convictions Determine Conduct" (2014). http://rickwarren.org/devotional/english/our-convictions-determine-conduct accessed May 24, 2016.

Willard, Dallas. *The Divine Conspiracy: Rediscovering Our Hidden Life in God.* New York: HarperCollins Publishers, 1998.
_________________. *Renovation of the Heart: Putting on the Character of Christ.* Colorado
Springs: NavPress, 2002.
_________________. *The Spirits of the Disciplines.* San Francisco: Harper Collins, 1999.
_________________ "My Journey To and Beyond Tenure in a Secular University." (2003).
http://www.dwillard.org/biography/tenure.asp accessed April 17, 2014.

__________________, "Spiritual Formation in Christ: A Perspective on What it is, and How it Might be Done" (2006). http://www.dwillard.org/articles/printable.asp?artid=81 accessed April 16, 2014.

__________________. "Spiritual Formation and the Warfare between the Flesh and Human Spirit" *Journal of Spiritual Formation and Soul Care* Vol. 1, No. 1 (2008): 79-87.

__________________, "Spiritual Formation: What it is, and How it is Done" (2009). http://www.dwillard.org/articles/printable.asp?artid=58 accessed April 15, 2014.

__________________ "Spiritual Formation as a Natural Part of Salvation." (2009) http://www.dwillard.org/articles/printable.asp?artid=135 accessed April 15, 2014.

Williamson, H.G. M. "Promises, Promises! Some Exegetical Reflections on Isaiah 58." *Word & World* Volume XIX, Number 2 (Spring 1999): 153-160.

Willis, John T. "Mediating Conditional and Unconditional Promises." *Restoration Quarterly* 54:1 (2012): 39-47.

YOUR NOTE: